BAD BRAINS TALES

BOOK TWO

THE CXNTERBURY TALES

MICK N BAKER

To Chris, Jess and Abbie

For Mum and Dad
With life comes understanding

.

Bad Brains Tales: Book Two
The Cxnterbury Tales

"Life is short. Art long.
Opportunity is fleeting.
Experience treacherous.
Judgement difficult."

— **Geoffrey Chaucer**

Chapter 1

Punk and Piss Orderly

People used to tell me that 'your school days are the best days of your life' which led me to believe that their post school years must have been really miserable. When I left school, I had wondered why churches across the country weren't ringing out in celebration; and since my departure, nothing I had seen, had changed my mind about it. I was now free to do whatever I wanted to do, and within a couple of months, both my mates Whiff and Andy were too, as the school year ended, and they broke up for the summer holidays. It was the freedom that I had craved, for over three years. We didn't want to waste a minute of it, so every chance we had, we practised, and at least now with Whiff in the band, we were all going in the same direction.

I felt like we had taken a step backwards, though, we were nowhere near the standard we were before and playing live seemed further away than ever, but Whiff was doing his best to put that right. In fact, Whiff was not only turning out to be a solid bass player and a good laugh, he was also someone you could have a decent conversation with, so it wasn't long before he started hanging out in the village with me and my mates, who despite his Gulliver like size, soon warmed to, the most of the time, gentle giant.

On the rare occasion when one of us had a few quid in our pocket, we used The Anchor, which was one of four pubs in the village; the others being: The Sow and Pigs, The Feathers and Windmill. It was very competitive in the village where pubs were concerned, so to make a living, Stewart, The Anchor's landlord, turned a blind eye to us underage drinkers, that is, as long as we didn't disturb his regular customers, who were a rowdy bunch anyway.

I had been drinking in The Anchor with Dave, Craig, and Simon 'Taddy' Ash since I was fifteen. Once we knew we would be served regularly, we had taken over the small lounge bar at the side of the pub, as not only was it out of the way of the main bar, but it had a dartboard, a bar billiards table, and its own serving hatch. Craig, Taddy, Dave and me would get a few funny looks when we first walked in, but as the night wore on and the drinks flowed, the regulars would relax; come into 'the nursery' as they called it, and have a laugh with us. A lot of them said they liked to see us in there as we added to the atmosphere of the place. On the not so-rare occasion that we were skint, we would stroll around the village, see who was about and what was going on, and most of the time, we would usually find something to get into.

One warm summer's evening, Whiff, Andy, and me were striding down Ermine Street, under a candy floss sky, when we heard the steady thump of music coming from Tarnia Gordon's house, one of the posher one's at the bottom near Old Church Lane. I had almost known Tarnia Gordon from my days back in The Thundridge Junior Mental Institution, and although it must have been at least five years since I had seen her standing on the other side of the playground, avoiding Kev, Trotsky and me, I thought there might be a chance of some free booze.

I pointed towards the thumping mansion, "Who wants to try and gate crash?"

Andy sniggered like Dick Dastardly's canine sidekick Muttley.

Whiff nodded, "Yeah, it's worth a try." His eyes, twinkling with mischief.

Andy, Whiff and me walked up to the huge property and wiped our muddy D.M.s on the tartan doormat, making an effort to clean ourselves up a bit. Effort made, I battered the urn door knocker on the dark mahogany door and stood back, fixing a pleasant smile onto my face.

A moment later, the heavy door swung in to reveal an excited, expectant Tarnia, who's eyes fell upon us, and she froze.

I beamed my fixed smile at her, "Hi Tarnia, how are you?"

Tarnia looked at me questioningly, her brow furrowing, then a dim light flicked on. "Oh yes err… Michael… how are you? Sorry, you've changed a bit." She said, examining my black bondage trousers, the zips, the straps, the D rings, the bum flap.

I smiled, "Yeah so have you, you look amazing," I simpered.

"Oh, thanks Michael" she laughed, clearly flattered.

I learnt around her, looking into the massive house, "What's going on here, it looks good."

Tarnia smiled proudly. "Yes, it is, it's my sixteenth birthday, I'm having a party," she trilled, fiddling with her necklace.

Andy grinned, "It looks like fun."

"Oh yeah, sorry Tarnia, where's my manners, this is Andy and that's Paul."

Whiff chuckled, "People call me Whiff, though."

"Oh, … Right…OK," she said, looking him up and down.

"Ah yeah, his second name is Hammersmith, it's nothing to do with his personal hygiene," I explained.

Andy snorted, "No, it's everything to do with his personal hygiene."

Tarnia cracked up laughing, so ceasing the moment, I flashed her another winning smile. "It's boring around here, isn't it? Can we come in for a while?"

Tarnia smiled, still amused at Andy's joke, she began fiddling with her necklace again, thinking.

A silver St Christopher spun round and round like it was deciding our fate, as she tried to make her mind up. I felt a chilling presence nearby and looked to the bay window and saw Tarnia's grandma, Mrs. Sampson or the Soup Dragon as we used to call her, when she served us our dinners at the Junior Mental Institution with her face perpetually set to miserable. The Soup Dragon's face clouded over like a British summer as it dawned on her that Tarnia might be about to let these louts into her lovely house and with a determined nod, she steeled herself and disappeared, leaving the bay window a lot easier on the eye.

I thought shit, she is going to head us off at the pass, so I stepped forward off the now filthy door mat onto the doorstep and played my trump card.

"Happy birthday Tarnia, we won't stay long," I said walking through the door.

Tarnia smiled making way, "Yes, yes, why not? Come in, come in, the more, the merrier."

"Why not, indeed," said Andy, following close behind me.

"OK, if you follow me, the party's in the lounge," she said, turning to lead the way.

Inside now, Tarnia led us down a long corridor, over ornate tiles of black and orange terracotta into a hall of luxurious Persian rugs. As we approached the lounge, I braced myself for the inevitable and inevitably the Soup Dragon stepped out in front of us, blocking our passage.

"Oh hello Mrs. Sampson," I smarmed, pleasantly.

"Oh hello… Michael," she spat tersely, accentuating the 'M'. Her face, that of thunder, her arse, that of a pregnant hippo.

I recoiled from her, like someone had put a freshly laid piece of dog shit under my nose and turned back to our host, knowing who was in charge, for tonight anyway.

"It's a lovely house, Tarnia, isn't it? Which way's the party again?"

"Aw thank you, that's very kind of you it's… Through there, in the lounge."

"Ah cheers, nice one, thank you."

"I might see you later then," Tarnia said with a wink.

I nodded graciously, smiling at Andy and Whiff, who grinned back, I then smirked at the smited dragon, and we sauntered off into the lounge to get some free booze.   ·

In the lounge, Soft Cell's 'Tainted Love' whined out from a stereo system in the corner of the white high-ceilinged lounge and by the time we had got to the middle of the room, there were nudges, laughter and smirking from the assembled groups of Soul boys, New Romantics and Yuppies.

One girl didn't even bother to hide her amusement, pointing at the wandering weirdos invading her party, she threw her head back, laughing like a hyena.

What the fuck are you laughing about, I thought, the padded shoulders on your suit jacket make you look like an American football player, and as for your princess Diana hair-cut, why would anyone want to look like that fucking doe eyed parasite?

"Whoaooo tainted love oohhh oooh…" sang Whiff directly into my earhole, bringing me back from my internal rant.

"It's no wonder it's tainted, he's as bent as arseholes," I said, lashing out at the poor sodomite.

"Have you heard that rumour about him?" Asked Andy.

"Marc Almond?" I said.

"I'll be buggered if I know who Marc Almond is," said Whiff.

"Yeah, that's him, the human milk churn," I said, in fits of Laughter.

Whiff cackled, shaking his head in disgust, "Euuurgh, come on, let's get pissed. Where's the drink?"

A huge tower of cans, bottles and wine boxes stood near the stereo, enticing us over, so without further ado, we barged our way across the large room and got stuck in.

A few pints of snakebite later, the world was looking a lot better, even Simon le bon's wank fest ode to some old prostitute he met in Brazil wasn't phasing me, even with its walking bass line of, 'Doom dee doom dee. Doom dee doom dee'.

Whiff serenaded us, as we poured the free drink down our throats. "Her name is Rio, and she costs about a pound," he warbled.

The human league followed in Whiff's twisted hit parade. "You used to work as a cock in a waitress tale bar," he crooned.

Kajagoogoo's 'too shy' came on, he threw his arms up, "Nah, I can't do that one, that's the top of the plops."

"Thank fuck for that, let's get out of here, have a look about," I said, wiping my brow for effect.

I dossed out the American football player and her skinny wedge-headed boyfriend, as we navigated our way through the still amused throng of dancing party goers.

"Too shy, shy, hush, hush, eye to eye…"

A quick burst of speed and we left the lounge, entering another long corridor, which led us out of the back of the house, into the lavish grounds at the rear of the property.

7

Once we were out of earshot of DJ twat, we set ourselves up near a group of small buildings and were back to the business of knocking the free pints back.

In one of the buildings there was an outside toilet, as party goers went in, they were leaving their drinks perched on top of a small ledge that ran along the side of the building. A soul boy casually belched in our direction, placed his lager on the ledge and strutted off into the bog, dossing us out.

"Oh what, did you see that? Who the fucking hell does he think he is? Watch this." I ran over to the ledge, quick as a flash, pulled my dick out, grabbed his half empty pint, and topped it up for him.

A couple of minutes later, the guy came back out, picked up his almost full pint, tilted his head back and took a huge draft.

"You alright mate?" I said nonchalantly, giving him a nod.

A little surprised, he said "Yeah," and took another swig.

"It's a great party, happy birthday Tarnia," I said, raising my glass aloft.

"Happy birthday Tarniaaaa, the wine bar wondeerrrrrrrr!"

Soul boy puffed his chest out, sniffed loudly and strutted off like he was in with the punks, as his stomach began to digest my warm piss.

It was a good thing I didn't have any more piss left inside my bladder, as I would have actually pissed myself, then and there, I was laughing so much. It was the same for the others.

Whiff was rolling around on the grass, howling with laughter.

Andy was in an even worse state, crouching down, clutching at his sides in a vain attempt to stop the pain that was splitting him in two.

A couple of Simon le Bonn lookalikes appeared, sniffed at the punks, placing their drinks on the ledge and disappeared inside the toilet.

Whiff stood up. "I'll get these," he said, reaching for his fly.

On and on we went; we drank, we pissed, we contaminated. It was an addiction; we just couldn't stop ourselves from generously freshening up people's drinks with our homebrew until I saw someone I recognised.

"Nah not this one, I know her," I said putting my hand up, to stop an overkeen Andy.

Whiff eyed her lecherously, "Cor she's alright. Who's she?"

"Lucy Harrington, she's alright, isn't she?"

"What?" Whiff laughed. "Harrington! Harrington, what like the jackets skinheads wear?"

"Yeah, yeah, shut up," I said impatiently, trying to stop his rambling brain.

Whiff stood up, spread his arms wide and bellowed, "Harrington, HARRINGTON, skinheads, SKINHEADSSSS." Just as she walked out of the toilet.

"You alright Lucy?" I asked.

Lucy gave Whiff a sideways look, "Oh, hi Skinner, what are you doing here? I didn't know you knew Tarnia."

I pulled a grimace, "Er… I don't really."

Lucy laughed, "No, nor do I, I'm only here for a drink I'm getting another one now, you want one?" Hauling me in with her brown eyes.

"OK, yeah," I said, totally taken by surprise.

"I've been meaning to have a chat with you, my brother's told me you're OK, come on," she said, beckoning me with a dark purple nail.

I smiled a smug smile at my mates and got up to follow her slim body into the house.

"Skinhead Jacket, me, aaaaaarrrrrington!"

I threw Whiff a V sign over my shoulder, following her down the long corridor back towards the lounge and the glut of booze.

Lucy Harrington was my next-door neighbour but since her family had moved into the street a few years previously, we had hardly exchanged a word. It was a shame as I used to see her walking past my house most mornings on the way to get the coach to Presdales, the girls' school in Ware and even in her school uniform, I thought she looked good; Lucy looked even better tonight in her tight denim mini skirt, black stockings and high brown leather boots.

Seb, her older brother and me were mates, we used to get the same bus to school in the morning. He was a proper John Peel head, who liked any kind of music 'as long as it wasn't the rubbish in the charts', so we had plenty to talk about, and take the piss out of.

Once we had got our drinks, sat down and got comfortable, I found out that Lucy was exactly the same as Seb where music was concerned, she liked punk, indie, reggae, her favourite band 'at the moment' being The Only Ones, who I secretly thought were pretty good too.

I chugged my snakebite back, put the empty glass on the low glass table in front of us, "Ahhh there's no drink like a snakebite."

Lucy smiled, sweeping her long brown hair back, "Bloody hell Skinner, you really are here for the drink, aren't you?"

"Tarnia who?" I said, smiling broadly.

Lucy sank hers, wiped her purple lips, "Me too."

"OK, let's get some more then, there's plenty," I said, eyeing up the towers of booze.

Lucy's face suddenly clouded over, "Oh yeah, I meant to say earlier, be careful not to leave your drink unattended if you use the outside toilet. I heard that somebody's been pissing in the drinks."

I suppressed a laugh, "Yeah, I heard that."

A couple of drinks later, the shit music got louder in volume and as a consequence we moved in closer, making me think that, maybe there was a point to this soppy drivel after all.

My old man and her mum had been known to have the odd, over the back garden fence political debates now and again, so I asked what she thought about them.

Lucy laughed, theatrically rubbing her forehead, like she was trying to exorcise the memory, "It's so embarrassing, I just don't know what to do with myself, my Dad listens at the window, just in case it gets out of hand."

"Oh my god, really, I'm so sorry, once my old man starts, that's it, he can't stop himself, he's a political junkie, he gets his fixes twice a day, the six o'clock news and the nine o'clock."

She snorted, "We need a higher fence."

"I reckon an electric one, would be better…. Bzzzzzz," I said, shuddering like I'd just touched it.

She laughed, wiping her lips again, "Aww, I don't think it would stop them, even then."

"AARRRINTON! Where's my skinhead jacket?"

Both of us jumped, we turned, to see Whiff. Pint fixed in hand. Grin fixed on face.

"Ah, yeah, this is my mate, Whiff."

Lucy looked at him suspiciously.

Whiff gently held her stare, a smile playing at his lips, "Who's this then, Skinner, what's her name?"

"Whiff, this is Lucy."

"Lucy what, what's her second name?" He enquired, leaning forward, eyes twinkling.

I pulled my mouth tight to stop the rapidly building grin appearing on my face, "Lucy... Err... Er... Ahem... Harrington... Er..."

"What? Sorry, I can't hear you."

"Lucy Harrington," I said, finally

Whiff sniggered, glancing back over his shoulder into the crowded room and shouted "SKINHEADSSSSSS!"

It took her about half a second to catch on, then her whole expression changed.

Lucy scowled at Whiff, "Oh, yes, how amusing, well done."

Lucy gave me a caustic look of betrayal, got up, smoothing her skirt down, "I'm going to get a drink, you arseholes."

A backwards glance of daggers at Whiff, and she stormed off.

"Oh, nice one you prat; I could have been in there," I said, before bursting out laughing,

"I've lost me aaarrrington naah... where's me aaarrrington gone?"

Whiff pumped his fist chanting, "Skinheads, Skinheads, Skinheads, Skinheads."

I cracked up, looking around the party to see if anyone else was laughing, saw people pairing off and my laugh froze in my throat.

"Nah I could have been in there mate, she was nice, funny too… And I got the green light from her older brother. You know what he said to me?"

"What's his name, Ben?"

"What!? No, it's Seb. What are you on about Whiff?"

"Ben Sherman Harrington."

I laughed, "Oh for fuck's sake," covering my eyes.

"OK, what did Ben, sorry I mean Seb, say?"

I sighed, "Nah you won't believe this mate, he said, and I quote 'if I wanted to, I could get my toe in there'."

Whiff pulled a face, "URGH… he said that about his little sister, the dirty bastard."

"I know, it's weird, isn't it? If I had a sister, I would look out for her," I said shaking myself like I was freezing.

Whiff didn't respond.

"Where's Andy?" I asked. "I haven't seen him since we were pulling piss pints."

Whiff grinned, "I left him alone, he's been chatting up some girl in the garden."

Oh, nice one mate, I thought, you leave him alone, so you can come and hassle me.

"Yeah, she's well tasty, he's been with her since you left. Come on, I'll show you, follow me."

"Oh what. No, No, No… Oh, Jesus!"

Whiff was already on his way, so I jumped up, following him back down the long corridor, dodging snogging couples as we went. I passed the American football player crumpled in a heap, sobbing, with a group of girls around comforting her, I couldn't help smiling to myself.

In the garden at the back of the house, couples were kissing, slow dancing and there, at the bottom of the grounds, lit up under a brace of floodlights, stood Andy, his arm around a short blonde girl.

Andy saw us coming, and quickly led his new friend in the opposite direction, disappearing through the white five bar gates at the bottom of the grounds.

"Whey, see?" Said Whiff, hurrying towards them.

"No, no come on, leave him to it mate, let's see if there's any more drink about," I said, trying to distract him.

15

Whiff burped, thunderously, rocking backwards, "Yeah, good idea, there's nothing left in the house though."

Whiff stopped, grinned, pointing at the pints lined up on the ledge of the outside toilet, "What do you reckon?" He said picking one up.

"I don't know."

Inspecting it like a wine taster, he rocked it to and fro, sniffing at it tentatively.

"Euuurgh, go on then, have a swig, I dare you," I said screwing up my face.

Whiff snorted, "I will if you do." Holding another glass out to me.

"Nah, fuck off, I'm not playing piss Russian Roulette, especially if it's with your piss."

He laughed, "What about the wine? Did we piss in the wine?"

"Well, I didn't, I'm a gentleman. What about you?"

Whiff smiled, "Of course I did."

"Come on, fuck this, let's try the house," I said, giving up.

Piss Pils and Piss Prosecco piss left behind us, we strolled back in through the back door and heard The Ruts single 'Babylon's Burning' blaring out from the front room.

"Bloody hell, what happened to Simon le mal?" I asked, following Whiff into the lounge.

Whiff walked over, greeted a bloke in red tartan bondage trousers, who was steadily nodding his head from behind the stereo system.

"Marcus, I didn't know you knew Talhia Corden?" Shouted Whiff.

"Who? I don't, I'm only here for the booze," he said, steadily watching the seven-inch disc spinning.

"Er... her names Tarnia Gordon, Whiff" I told him.

Whiff turned on me, "Talhia Corden!! Yeah, I know, that's what I said."

I nodded; I couldn't be bothered.

"I see you brought a few records with you too?" He said getting back to Marcus.

Marcus nodded wisely, "It's a necessity these days, with the coming of the New Romanpricks there's so much shit around."

Whiff and Marcus 'Mucus' Crosswell were good mates, knew each other from Shit-Shore school, so I stood back listening, letting them talk, Whiff told him there was no booze left and warned him about the piss cocktails sitting on the ledge of the outside toilet, which had him in stitches.

Mucus cued up 'H eyes' by The Ruts, his next offering in the alternative hit parade, and while Malcolm Owen warned the kids of the dangers of heroin, Mucus told us that when he arrived, he had stashed a party four of cider in the under stairs' cupboard, 'for emergencies just like these', so I volunteered to retrieve them. Whiff wished me luck on my quest for the precious alcohol, and I set off.

I slouched nonchalantly up the ornately tiled corridor towards the stairs, passing the patrolling Soup Dragon, who looked at her watch huffily, tutting as she went by.

Bollocks this party isn't over yet, I thought, quickly collecting the precious tinies, and by the time I got back to the lounge, the UK Subs single 'Stranglehold' was blaring out of the stereo.

"Hey presto," said I, revealing the tins from inside my studded leather jacket, like a magician, then distributed to the eager outstretched hands in front of me.

Andy came bursting into the room, grinning like the Cheshire Cat, and walked straight up to me, holding my stare, jabbing his middle finger right under my nose.

One sniff is all it took; it was that familiar fanny smell, seeing the recognition register on my face he absolutely cracked up laughing.

Whiff lurched forward, "What? What? What?"

Andy pressed his fingers under Whiff's nose.

Whiff sniffed, re-sniffed, sniffed again, and it dawned on him, his face broke into raucous laughter.

"Andy put his pinky in the stinky, he put his pinky in the stinky," He chanted, cracking up.

All of us joined in with the chant, while Andy passed his finger around, like it was doing a lap of honour, smiling broadly after each sniff.

A short blonde girl with a group of mates, followed by the Soup Dragon, entered the room, Andy's face froze, and the heroic finger disappeared into his pocket.

"Is this them, Sandra?" The Soup Dragon asked.

"Yes, those three," she said, pointing accusingly.

"I think you'd better go now," she said, simmering with rage, simmering with absolute delight thrown in.

"What? Has all the beer gone?" Whiff asked, grinning at the rest of us.

"I think that's very rude," said The Soup Dragon, eyeing this miscreant.

"I'm sorry, I didn't mean that," said Whiff.

She nodded, self-righteously, and opened her mouth to continue her self-righteousness.

"Yeah, but I didn't mean that either," Whiff cut in.

All of us creased up laughing.

"Leave now, or I'll call the police," she said furiously, her face turning puce.

"If you're going to call the police, you must make sure to use a telephone, or they won't be able to hear you from here," Whiff taunted.

"Oh, they'll hear me alright, don't you worry about that," she threatened.

"OK, we'll go, but I'm not going anywhere until I've said goodbye to Talhia Corden."

"And who in god's name is she?" Trilled the Soup Dragon.

"Oh what, it's her birthday party, don't you know that?" Said Whiff, conclusively.

"OUT, OUT, GET OUT, GET OUT!" Screeched the Soup Dragon, losing it totally.

"OK, OK, come on let's go, we know when we're not wanted," I said sounding hurt.

Whiff, Andy and me turned and sauntered out to the sounds of 'Disease' by The UK Subs, the Soup Dragon, close by, shadowing us until we were out of her house, put out onto the street.

The Soup Dragon slammed the door victoriously behind us, the bang of the solid mahogany door echoing off the house opposite and back again, like an angry call and response.

"What was that all about?" I asked Andy.

"I told Sandra we had been pissing in the drinks," Andy admitted, looking down.

Whiff cackled, "Was that before or after you fingered her?"

Andy gave him a withering look, "Well obviously after, Whiffy."

"Sorry I couldn't resist, why did you tell her, though?" Whiff said, intrigued.

"I don't know really, she told me that her and her mates had been drinking the wine, and they thought it tasted off like the bottles had corked, whatever that means, so I just said no we've been pissing in the drinks all night."

"And she must have told the old bag?" I said finishing for him.

Andy nodded sadly.

I put a placating hand on his shoulder, patting him, "Ah don't worry about it Andy, they took the piss out of us when we arrived, and we gave them some piss back, and they didn't like it, so what, bollocks to them."

"Yeah, don't worry Andy, the party was over anyway," said Whiff, grinning.

Whiff stopped and grabbed Andy, "Oi, give us a go on that finger again."

"I'm never going to wash my hands after that," Andy announced, sticking his middle finger up in the air, showing it off to the world.

Whiff, Andy and me sauntered back up Ermine Street, the sound of our raucous laughter echoing back and forth off the houses, like a light-hearted call and response as we went.

Chapter 2

Bobby Charlton's Comb Over

Whiff's place in the band was secure after Tarnia Gordon's party, as not only was it a good laugh, more importantly, we had backed each other up when it had counted; it was his rite of passage and now the past was just that. We were united, we were stronger, we were moving on.

On the Friday night before our next practice, Dave solved another problem for us, a problem we had right from the start. I was struggling across the A10 in front of his house, underneath my Laney amp, when a horn blasted out, making me pitch forward haphazardly. I turned, ready to give the horn blower the wankers sign, and there was Dave beaming at me from behind the wheel of a van, parked up on the forecourt of the all-night garage. It was a Ford Marina, sprayed yellow, with AD Builders written in black on the side; A for Alan, Dave's old man and D for Dave. I struggled over to him beaming back, put my amp down, thinking, hoping that we wouldn't have to lug our gear down to the pavilion anymore.

Dave jumped out and punched the air. "I passed," he shouted.

I pumped my fist back, "Yessss… well done mate, I didn't know you were having another driving test?"

"I didn't tell anyone this time; I didn't want to jinx it."

"Good idea, mate," I nodded appreciatively, at his logic, "It looks alright, doesn't it?"

"Yeah, and take a look at this, Skin. It's just what we've been waiting for."

I followed him around the back, he flipped open the twin doors, "Look at this, there's plenty of room for the band's gear in here."

I leant forward, ducking my head down to get a better look, and peered inside, thinking it was absolutely perfect for us, it was what we've been waiting for. Dave's drums can go…

"BAKER!"

I jumped up, banging my head on the roof, spun round and saw Alan, Dave's old man, coming towards us from under the carport, a massive smile creasing up his face.

"You should've seen your face, Baker, you jumped out of your Skin… you wouldn't have got on with my old drill sergeant!" Alan said, and to illustrate he shouted, "LEFT RIGHT, LEFT RIGHT, MOOOOOVE, YOU 'ORRIBLE H'OBJECTS."

Alan cracked up laughing, and we both joined him, as when Alan laughed, it was like his whole face lit up, it was impossible not to follow suit.

Once we had all stopped laughing, we turned our attention back to the new van.

I said, "It's alright, isn't it?"

Alan nodded, scratching his chin thoughtfully, "Hmm… not bad."

"What is it?" I asked.

"It's a Ford Marina, good little runners they are."

"How many miles on the clock?"

"Bloody hell, he knows all the questions, doesn't he?" Alan glanced at Dave, eyebrows raised.

Alan looked back to the van, slowly shaking his head from side to side "Baker…" he said, chuckling to himself.

"David, did you see Hayley while you were driving around?" Asked Alan, shaking the menace of Baker from his mind.

"No," Dave replied.

Alan let out a sigh, like a burst tyre, "Bloody hell, she asked me to take her to Ware. Now she's disappeared off the face of the bloody Earth."

Dave and me looked at each other, keeping our smiles in check.

"I'm waiting for her! Bloody hell, she asked me, and I'm waiting for her… and I'm paying for the bloody petrol too…"

"It sounds like someone's being stitched up," I said poignantly.

Alan absolutely creased up laughing, "You got that right, Skinner." He repeated, "Sounds like someone's being stitched up," laughing again.

"If you ever have a family Skinner, God forbid, never have girls. Boys will look after themselves, but girls… bloody hell, you've got to look after them forever."

I smiled, nodded and with one more mirthful whisper of 'sounds like someone's being stitched up' Alan crossed the road, shading his eyes from the late evening sunshine and began to look up and down the A10, looking for any sign of his errant daughter.

I looked back to Dave.

"Let's mooove… Baker," he Alan-ed.

"Bloody hell, mate, have a heart," I Alan-ed back.

I carefully lofted my amp into the back of the van, making sure it sat on one of the dust sheets, while Dave disappeared into his house, returning a moment later with his bass drum case, and together we placed it tight up against my amp.

Alan strode back across the road and paused in front of us. He took one last hopeful look up and down the road, seeing nothing and no one.

"Standing here like a cunt," he said and marched off back under the carport.

I hadn't heard an adult say that word before. I snorted, looked to Dave, who was also trying to hold his laughter back, the kitchen door slammed shut behind Alan, and then we fell about laughing.

A few easy minutes later, the van was packed, ready to go, so we set off down the A10, turned first left onto the gravel track and immediately began to bounce and pitch as the van negotiated the harsh potholes. At the end of the gravel track, I got out, opened the gate next to the allotments, and we drove down the long, sweeping hill that led to the pavilion. Dave hit the brakes, stopping us just before we got onto the grass area that surrounds the football and cricket pitches.

"I've got some bad news. We're not allowed to drive on the grass, we've got to park here and hump the gear over," said Dave, staring irately at the two-hundred yards that separated us from the pavilion.

"Oh, fucking hell!" I said, slapping my forehead.

"Oh, fucking hell indeed," Dave replied.

"Or maybe not," he said, ramming the van into first. "Hold on tight!"

Dave stamped on the accelerator, we shot forward across the grass, our gear shifting perilously in the back and as the pavilion came hurtling towards us, he wrenched up the hand brake, sending us into an uncontrolled skid, and we broadsided across the grass, eventually coming to a gliding halt near the pavilion entrance.

I looked at Dave, he gave me the thumbs up grinning back, and we burst into fits of laughter. "You're a nutter, you are!"

Dave nodded, grabbed the door handle, got out and his face fell flat. "Oh shit… Look at that," he said, gawking at two ten feet gouge marks in the grass behind the van.

"Ah they won't notice that it's fine," I said, calmly.

"They will Skin," he insisted, dropping to his knees, frantically, Dave began pushing blades of grass into the gouges like some kind of crazy Bobby Charlton comb over.

"Come on, help me!" He cried.

I dropped down next to him, laboriously combing over the grass, and unsurprisingly, just like Bobby Charlton's infamous cover up, it was fooling nobody.

"Hold on," I said, thinking.

I walked over to the long grass at the edge of the pavilion, dragged out a couple of big tufts, roots and all, dropped them into the gouges and tamped them down with my feet.

"Yeah, that's a good idea," Dave said as he went and got some clumps for himself.

Once we had finished, we stood back to admire our handy work, and saw that the grass we had planted into the gouges was too long, so Dave fetched a pair of pliers from the works van, gave them a quick trim up, and we stood back again. It was seamless, so we unloaded the van, had one of our unofficial practices', ending our evening with a few quiet pints in The Anchor.

*

On Saturday morning, I went to Dave's and was just about to knock the door when Anne, Dave's mum, saw me through the kitchen window and waved me in. I waved, wandered through the lean-to, and into the kitchen where Anne was peeling potatoes with a huge carving knife.

28

"You don't need to knock Michael, just come straight in," She said, kindly.

"Thanks, is Dave ready?" I asked.

Anne nodded ominously towards the dining room.

Dave was standing, head down, looking uncomfortable.

"Bloody hell, mate, I've just had Reg bloody Cooper round here telling me all about the world," Alan stormed.

I looked to Anne, "What's happened? Is there anything wrong?"

Anne gave me a withering look, sighed loudly and got back to brutalising her spuds.

Dave saw I had come in, grimaced, and then Alan's head appeared around the door.

"Ah, here he is, the other one… How long have you been lugging those amplifiers down to the pavilion, Skinner?" Alan questioned.

Oh shit, I thought to myself, catching on, "I don't know. About a year?"

"And you get a chance to make life easy for yourselves, and what do you do? You ruin it," Alan said, shaking his head, turning back to Dave.

Ann shook her head, "Silly, silly, boys… If it weren't for Alan, you wouldn't be practising in the pavilion anymore." She repeated, "Silly, silly boys." Decapitating another spud.

Dave sighed expansively, "Come on, Skin, let's wait for Whiff and Andy outside."

Alan let out a huge sigh, "Bloody old boys," followed us out of the kitchen.

Once we had got under the carport at the front of the house, Dave filled me in on the morning's events. Reg Cooper had seen our poor attempt to cover the skid marks with 'yellow grass' straight away, pulled the tufts out, saw our gear in the pavilion, put two and two together and marched up to Dave's to have it out with Alan. Dave reckoned that he could hear the furious grounds man going on from up in his bedroom, apparently, he had been demanding that we should be banned with immediate effect. Alan had stuck up for us though, saying that it was just high spirits, everybody makes mistakes when they are young, surely, we should have a second chance. In the end thankfully, Reg Cooper had compromised agreeing that we could carry on practising at the pavilion but as a punishment we would have to park up next to the allotments at the top of the hill and hump our gear down from there; all in all, I thought it was a good result.

"It's fine Skin, don't worry it, we'll do it for a couple of weeks then we'll drive it down again," Dave said, making it even better.

I nodded, "OK mate, if you're sure."

Whiff and Andy showed up a bit later, squeezed themselves, sardine like, into the back of the van, in amongst our gear, and we set off for a shorter than planned ride to the allotments.

As we drove slowly pitching up and down on the gravel track, Dave told them what had happened the night before and the aftermath this morning, making both of them crack up.

"You almost got us banned, for driving on the grass?" Asked Whiff, smirking.

Dave nodded, spinning the wheel to avoid another deep crater, "Yeah, pretty much."

Andy sang, "Banned from the pavilion OK, we did like playing there anyway," paraphrasing Crass' Banned from the Roxy track.

Once we had stopped laughing, all of us agreed that it had been a massive overreaction by Reg Cooper; that was until we had walked about half-way down the hill and saw the two massive brown skid marks cutting right across the centre of the cricket pitch.

"Bloody hell, look at that," I said, unbelievingly.

"Jesus Christ, no wonder he got the hump," Dave said.

"It looks like your skiddy kecks Whiffy," Andy joked.

"That's a bit harsh, isn't it?" I asked.

"Harsh realities of life, my friend," said Andy, coming back with the standard reply.

Whiff retorted, "Oi you're skid mark central Andy, you're like the Dunlop of skid marks."

Andy laughed, "Dun-plop pants, Whiffy"

I listened to them go backwards, forwards, forwards, backwards, for a while, then I gave the whole sorry misadventure some proper thought. It wouldn't necessarily have been the end of Virus V1, it would have just been another obstacle for us to find our way around. Dave could drive now, so we go anywhere, well anywhere within reason. I knew of a place in Ware, which was tailor-made for bands like us, the only thing was, we would have to pay by the hour and with Dave being the only one of us in full-time employment, we hardly ever had any money. In the end, I was relieved to be staying on at the pavilion. It had been our home for a year, we liked it there, we felt settled, and we could do what we wanted… Well, apart from doing hand brake turns on the cricket pitch, that is.

Once we had stopped laughing about Dave's grass skid marks and Whiff and Andy's shitty skid marks, we lashed through our twelve-track set, finishing on one of our favourites, V1 Bomb. I put my guitar down to make a roll up and as my fingers deftly put it together, I looked around the pavilion at everyone, talking, laughing, getting on, and I thought we are better now than we have ever been, not only because we are better musicians, meaning we are tighter as a band, we are all mates, who are going in the same direction, enjoying what we are doing.

On top of that, despite our best efforts to fuck it up, we had finally sorted out our transport problems. It was time now, we were ready, ready to play live. Andy and Whiff were part of a small but dedicated punk scene, which flourished around their native Ware and Hertford town, so I asked them to put some feelers out to see if there were any gigs coming up; I didn't have to wait long.

*

A few nights later, I was sitting in the lounge, watching That's Life on TV with mum and the old man, when the phone rang, giving the old man a start and he gave mum a worried look. In our house, the phone ringing was a rare occurrence, it only meant one thing as far as he was concerned, bad news, he had only had it put in for emergencies.

"I'll get it," I announced and padded off to the phone in the hall.

I parroted, "Hello, Ware double six one double six," as my old man had instructed.

It was Andy. "I've got some good news; we've got our first gig!"

A small kaleidoscope of butterflies took flight in my stomach, which I quickly swatted away, thinking, this is it, this is what we've been working towards for the last year. In the wake of the retreating butterflies, an enormous feeling of excitement fluttered through me.

"Oh, nice one, Andy! Where is it?" I asked.

Andy chuckled. Pausing for effect, "I'm not sure you're going to like this Skinner… It's at Richard Hale school."

"Oh ha, ha, well done very good, tell us about it mate?" I said, not falling for that one.

"No, it is, I promise you, we're supporting Onslaught, Matt plays drums for them, you know Bean's little brother… It's a CND benefit."

I looked into the fisheye mirror on the opposite wall and saw my distorted face boggling back.

"It looks like you're going back to Richard Hole after all, Skinner."

"Oh, fucking hell… Nah… It's brilliant mate. It's about time they had some decent music there!" I said, recovering.

Andy confirmed the details, hung up, and I strolled back into the lounge, smiling broadly.

"What was that all about?" The old man asked cautiously, fearing the worst.

"Ah, it's nothing really, well… We've got a gig," I said, as casually as I could.

Mum clasped her hands together, absolutely delighted. "Oh, that's great news, Mike, well done!"

"Hmmm," said the old man, raising his eyebrows.

"It's good news, isn't it, Pudge?" Mum said, turning to him.

"Yeah," he said, turning his attention back to Esther Rantzen's plunging neckline.

Chapter 3

Back In the Jug Agane

On the evening of our first gig, Dave and me loaded up the gear into his van and set off for Richard Hole School, the place I swore I would never return to. I sat back on the unforgiving black, plastic seat and watched the over familiar, non-landmarks passing by my window. In Ware, the grey viaduct of the A10 bypass, the old, dilapidated library, which in the winter housed lonely grannies trying to keep warm, and finally the thief's paradise Boots the chemists on Ware high street. In Hertford, the huge, foreboding police station with its ominous array of antennae on its roof, watching, monitoring. The cattle market, where pigs, sheep and cows were sold for slaughter and finally the post office ran by a Pakistani family who were always getting their windows smashed because they came from Pakistan. I thought that it was the ultimate irony that our first gig was at Richard Hole, as it was the place that had galvanized my hatred for not only the educational system, but society as a whole. I nodded to myself, satisfied in the knowledge that the first line of the first track we were going to play at Richard Hole school tonight was 'Fuck the State', then I got back to my non-sightseeing; fuck the state, indeed.

In through the front entrance, up past the tennis courts, around the main buildings, Dave drove us, pulling up with a screech outside the main hall, the scene of my last O level examination. Andy saw us through the windows of the main hall and disappeared behind one of the curtains. The main doors flew open, and he came bounding over to us, a big smile on his face.

"You alright Skinner? Alright Dave?" He asked, leaning into my open window.

35

"Yeah, sort of, I can't believe I'm back here again," I replied.

Andy grinned, "I can, I was here about twenty-four hours ago."

I laughed, "Oh you poor sod, that's sad."

Andy nodded, "I wonder if Percy Penrose is coming."

"Who?" Enquired Dave.

"He's one of our music teachers, I can just see him po-go-ing down at the front," Andy said, laughing at the image.

I smiled, "I doubt it, I told him I played guitar once, and he asked, 'oh how lovely, classical?' and I said 'no, punk' and he looked at me like I'd just put my dick on his chin."

Dave slapped the steering wheel laughing, repeating, "Dick on his chin."

"Bloody hell Skin, that was subtle… Subtle as a brick." Andy replied.

"OK come on, let's get unloaded," Dave said, getting down to business.

Andy saluted, "Aye, aye, captain."

Once we had got all our gear into the main hall, we began setting up and even though the gig wasn't due to start for an hour or so, there were quite a few people in, talking, laughing, enjoying themselves, feeling the anticipation of the soon to begin gig. I wondered where Whiff was, he should have been here ages ago, I was going to ask

Andy if he knew where he knew was, then I thought better of it, he seemed to be having his own problems. He was leant forward over his mic, face red, a picture of frustration, twiddling its wire first left, then right, as it cut in and out when he spoke into it.

Oh, he'll be here, Whiff wouldn't miss our first gig, I thought, turning my attention to getting myself ready. I plugged my guitar into our tuner, flipped the on switch, only to watch the needle wave randomly backwards and forwards a couple of times, then die.

"Oh, fucking hell, why now?" I raged.

Andy looked up from his dodgy mic, "What's the matter?"

"Ahhh I don't know. Oh no, I think the fucking batteries are dead Andy," I said, taking the batteries out, warming them in my palm.

"Yeah and we'd better be more careful loading up next time," said Dave from behind us, holding up one of his mounted toms. "It's only got fucking split, hasn't it!"

Andy and me traipsed over, had a look, it looked bad.

Andy said, "Are you going to be able to play with it, like that Dave?"

"Yeah, yeah, it should be alright, might sound a bit weird though."

"Fucking great," I said, sarcastically.

"Oh well, at least you will make a sound, I won't, our microphone keeps cutting out," stated Andy dejectedly.

37

"I knew I shouldn't have come back here; Richard fucking Hole, this place is fucking jinxed," I said, shaking my head angrily.

"WAAAAAAAAAAAAAYYYYYYYYYY!" Yelled Whiff, peddling his mum's Bridgford priory ladies' heritage bike into the hall.

Andy, Dave and me immediately forgot all of our problems, dissolving into fits of laughter.

"Oh, hello Mrs. Hammersmith, and where's Paul today?" I opened with.

Andy Judy-ed, "Oh, Paul… You've stolen my bicycle."

I echoed, "Oh Paul." Covering my eyes with my hands. "Well, that's our street credibility gone then."

Dave paced backwards and forwards thwacking a drum stick off his head repeating, "He came on his mum's bike, he came on his mum's bike."

Whiff smiled, watching the clowns, quietly taking it all in his stride, finally he said, "What? What's up with it? It's a good bike, it really goes." A bit affronted.

Dave repeated, "It really goes?" Smirking.

"What, to the W.I?" I said, walking over to it. "Oh, for fucks sake, look at this, look at this…" I said incredulously pointing at the turtle motif, duck egg blue bell.

"TING, TING"

Dave and Andy fell about, while a nonplussed Whiff stood still, scanning our mirthful faces.

"I'm going to ride it to all of our gigs now," proclaimed Whiff.

"What gigs, there won't be any more gigs mate, our creds gone, its kaput, vamoosed," I said, laughing.

Dave Alan-ed, "Bloody hell mate, have a heart."

"If we're going to get the bike every time, then maybe we should get Judy to play bass for us," Andy jested.

Dave cackled, "Ah Jesus no, can you see her playing bass on 'Christ Fuckers'?"

"Oh Paul, you can fuck your own Christ," I Judy-ed

I thought this is just too good to miss, I shoved Whiff aside, grabbed the bike, jumped on and peddled off, ringing the turtle motif, duck egg blue bell as I went. I navigated my way, left then right, right then left through the throngs of people, who jumped out of the way creasing up, laughing at the knob end on a knob end's bike. A runway opened up in front of me at the top of the hall as people cleared out of the way, so I pelted back towards my howling mates, and as I closed in on them, I yanked the brakes on, pulling a decent broadside in front of them.

Dave and Andy stepped forward, grabbing at the bike.

"Let's have a go!"

"Me first!"

Whiff stood back, vindicated and let them have a go.

"See, it's not so bad," he said.

Once we had all taken duck egg blue for a couple of spins around the rapidly filling hall, we got back to setting up and everything seemed to fall into place.

Onslaught's drummer Matt sorted Andy and Dave out with some masking tape, curing their problems and I managed to rub a bit of life back into my tuner's battery, and we were ready. Richard Hale School's main hall had certainly seen more people in the past, but as we walked onto the stage, I thought it was a decent turn-out for our first gig. Whiff checked his bass was in tune for the fourth time, Dave warmed up doing a series of paradiddles on the snare, Andy was upright, ready, so I hit a couple of chords, asked 'OK?' and they looked back slightly apprehensive, nodding in the affirmative.

Dave let loose the intro for our opening number 'Everybody's Boy', hit a quick snare roll, and we all came in on time, and that was it, we were now playing our first gig.

A group of people down the front were nodding their heads getting into it, a few more at the back were jumping around, pogo-ing, then from nowhere there were two blokes up on stage with us, grabbing and pushing into each other. Andy rushed forward, pushed them, steaming in hard, one stumble backwards, arms reaching out for some kind of balance, the other almost fell head first off the stage onto the floor. Nah Andy, don't do that mate, I thought, what's the problem? It's a punk gig, it's going to get rough, if someone wants to shout abuse or get up on the stage, as long as they aren't interfering with us playing, then fair enough. It's angry music, people are

40

supposed to get angry. I was proved right by the time the second chorus came, it was like something had been switched off in the audience, the people at the front, who had been nodding their heads, were now standing statuesque, staring maliciously at us, at Andy, in particular. One of the blokes who had been bounced offstage was pointing and shouting abuse at him, so I blew the little twat a sweet kiss, got back doing what we were here for, making a decent fucking racket, hoping they would get back to what they had been doing, jumping around. A coke can shot across the floor under me, putting me up onto one leg, looking up for the culprit, I saw a whole hall full of possibilities.

In amongst the tide of anger that was washing over us, I saw a lone foot tapping perfectly along with our beat, I thought oh well, at least someone's enjoying it, then I realised that it was Dave's foot on the high hat, and I thought you have got to get a grip here.

A massive shot of adrenaline rushed through my veins when it came to my solo on 'Everybody's Boy', my hands seemed to take on a life of their own, running up the neck of the guitar like a spider, settling on four random strings.

I hit it as hard as I could; it sounded shit.

I watched the spider scamper further up the neck, grabbing another four strings.

I hit it as hard as I could; it sounded even worse than shit, I began to think that maybe the twat at the front bellowing you're shit at me, might have a point.

Dave's full kit drum roll brought the curtain down on my first live guitar solo, one of the worst I had ever played, steering me back to the safety of the glorious Bar E.

A few cheers, some sporadic applause, greeted us at the end of 'Everybody's Boy', which surprised us, not the least Andy, who was still dossing out the attempted stage invaders, daring them to try it again. A massive shriek of feedback took Andy's attention away from errant front row, and he switched his mic off, killing it dead.

Dave hit the beat to our second track 'Christ Fuckers', Andy drew the mic up, ready to start the chant, on the second bar he sang nothing as the mic was still switched off. Andy spun around, making neck chopping signals to Dave who stopped playing, quickly turning it back on again, bringing more feedback.

In the whining feedback, clearly frustrated now, Andy blurted out, "Oh yes CND can organise gigs very well, can't they?"

"CND are a bunch of wankers," I said, feeling the frustration myself, backing up our vocalist.

In the audience, the tide of anger had now turned into a wave,

"Well fuck off then"
"You fucking wankers"
"You're shit"
"Smart, that was really smart"
"You cunt"
"Good going"
"Get another singer"

I thought this is just going from bad to worse, how can we carry on playing in front of this lot now, we've only played two tracks, and we've already pissed off most of the people here; we've got another ten tracks to play, we're going to get fucking lynched.

"Come on lads, fuck them, let's play," said Dave rallying us.

Dave smashed into the beat, putting his marker down, showing some true grit, and for the second time that day, I thought you have got to get a grip here, this what we've been working towards for a year, keep playing, see what happens, maybe it's not over yet.

Whiff gave me a nod of encouragement, clearly, he was feeling it too, I nodded back, thinking we're right behind you Andy, it's up to you now mate.

Andy chanted, "Symbol of religion, a man in pain, Jesus died well what a shame, so that we might be forgiven, sin is what we live in… You can fuck your own Christ."

Dave hit the snare roll, Whiff and me brought the wall of guitars in and once again, with the music playing, anything seemed possible.

Andy was absolutely belting it out, I didn't know it at the time, but he had been holding back at our practices, probably for moments just like these, I fed off it, I wasn't the only one, a couple of groups in the audience were beginning to nod along too. I scanned the audience, did a double take, near the back I saw Hair Bear Harper, his face unreadable under his long black curly hair. Next to him stood Gary Walsh, Simon Bamford and Matt Beresford, their faces totally readable, they were all grinning, bopping their heads, enjoying what they were hearing.

'Christ Fuckers' last notes faded, giving way to a decent smattering of applause, a few cheers and thankfully no more abuse, maybe the tide will turn I thought.

On our next track 'Protest', I played the first two bars on my own, holding down the last chord to fade and waited for Dave's drum roll to bring us all in.

"Ha, ha, you fucked it up," one of the stage invaders shouted victoriously.

I snorted, glanced at the fool, shook my head and Dave smoothly hit a snare tom combination roll, and it was lift off, just as he had rehearsed it a hundred times before.

People enjoyed the fast pace of 'Protest', nodding their heads to the beat, bouncing up and down, showing their appreciation. One minute thirty seconds later, when the track came to its end, they all clapped enthusiastically.

"Cheers, cheers, ta very much," said Andy, now completely ignoring his distractors.

It felt like we were beginning to win them over. I thought thank fuck for that, we liked our music, most of our mates liked it too, but there was nothing quite like watching people listening to your music for the first time and getting into it; playing our music was all well and good, but with nobody around to hear it, it was like a tree falling over in the wilderness.

Virus V1 played another six tracks with the faster tempo one's going down the best, so it was fitting that we finished on another fast one, our signature track V1 Bomb. Dave and me had worked particularly hard on that one at our unsanctioned Friday night practices to get it just right, both of us knowing it had great potential.

Dave hit the fast-paced military roll on the snare, building up and up in volume for two bars, I came in with a dampened guitar riff, then as the bar ended, Dave lashed out right across the kit in a full drum roll and then lift off, we all came in.

People started jumping around, the floor started pitching along with us, Andy felt the connection, bellowing our message out into the hall, pointing at some of his mates down the front, who in turn pumped their fists, pointing back at him; the tide had turned.

On the left of the stage Whiff also felt it, he lashed into his strings, exorcising the frustration that we had all been feeling, the floor trembling underneath him.

In the middle Dave was the king of the drum rolls, hitting the military rolls, building to a crescendo and me? I was loving every second of it, wasn't I.

A massive cheer went up as V1 Bomb ended and unbelievably, even some of the people who had been giving us a stick earlier, were asking for an encore.

I wondered if they were taking the piss, but so what if they were, some people wanted an encore, and we wanted to carry on playing now we were warmed up, so we did the first three tracks again, which went down a lot better the second time round, and we left the stage to the sound of cheering, applause, whistles and that was it, it was over, we had done it, our first gig.

One of the organizers pulled the stage curtains shut, and we wandered back on to pack our gear away to make way for the headliners, Onslaught.

Matt strolled over from the side of the stage, with Gary and Simon in tow, "You were pretty good," he said, nodding.

"Cheers, Matt, you sound surprised?"

Matt chuckled, "I was, you stopping to watch us?"

I looked around at the others, who nodded in the affirmative.

"Of course, mate, looking forward to it."

"If any wanker hassles Onslaught, they're going to get chinned," Gary stated.

Simon sighed expansively, giving me, a what can I do look.

I shrugged my shoulders, knowing some people will never change.

Matt offered, "You want a hand with your gear?"

"OK, nice one, if you're sure mate, cheers," I said, now I was surprised.

"One thing though…"

"What?" I said, expecting to see at least half of my bacci pouch disappear.

"Er… can I have a go on that bike?"

"Oh, fucking hell, don't encourage him," I said, looking at a now grinning Whiff.

"Yeah, OK," said Whiff cracking up.

"Go easy on the bell, though," he warned.

Matt laughed manically, rushing off to retrieve duck egg blue bell with its turtle motif.

Once we had got our gear and Whiff's mum's bike safely packed into the van, we stood back and watched Onslaught's set.

In between their raucous tracks I thought about, us, Virus V1, how we had proved some people wrong; we weren't shit. How we had proved some people right; we were shit; to be shit or not to be shit, that was the question? It was our first gig, I didn't know. One thing I did know was, that we had enjoyed ourselves, had a good laugh - Virus V1 were up and running, we were already looking forward to our next gig and where that would take us, as for Onslaught, I thought they were pretty good too.

Chapter 4

Who's That Siouxsie Girl?

A few weeks after the Richard Hole gig, Dave bought his first car, a silver Cortina 1600e, Dave and me were at his place admiring its sleek aerodynamic lines when Alan and Hayley appeared from under the car port.

"Oi, are you not in the army yet, Baker?" Alan asked, a smile erupting across his face.

Hayley snorted, "I doubt they'd want him, Dad."

"Oh, thank god for that," I said, wiping my brow theatrically, making Hayley's pretty face burst into an infectious laugh.

Dave's older sister Hayley seemed to have it all, good-looking, funny, intelligent and sometimes when she was about, you could quite easily believe you were with a girl off an early Woody Alan film, as underneath all that intelligence and charisma, she could be quite dippy sometimes, which just added to the attraction. I knew I would never be more than a friend to her though, as not only was she a few years older than me, meaning that she was a lot more confident and relaxed in her own skin, she was Dave's older sister, so she was totally out of bounds.

"I love this car, it's gorgeous, isn't it?" Hayley said, sweeping her long, blonde hair back.

"Yeah, it's beautiful," I agreed, looking at her long, blonde hair.

Alan nodded in agreement. "It's a nice motor, lovely bit of craftsmanship, and it's got the engine too, that'll shift," he grinned mischievously.

"Has it got A.B.S. on it?" I asked.

Alan rocked back on his heels, eyeing me suspiciously and said, "Bloody hell Skinner, have you been thumbing through the Exchange and Mart again?" His face creasing up.

"I bet you've got a subscription, haven't you Skinner? You never miss an issue," Hayley laughed.

"Thumbing through the exchange and mart," repeated Dave, wiping tears of laughter from his eyes.

"Do you want to get in, Skin?"

"Yeah," I said, pulling open the heavy, metallic, silver door.

I sunk into the sumptuous driver's seat, placing my hands on the racing steering wheel, looked at the road ahead and thought yeah, I could get used to this. I wasn't going anywhere though, I hadn't even had a driving lesson, so instead I checked out its plush interior. It was a world away from my old man's mustard coloured mini 850cc, with its harsh plastic seats, plastic dashboard and gaping hole to the road below under the near side passenger's seat.

In front of me, a series of dials mounted into a walnut dashboard surround shone back at me, in the middle, at the bottom of the silver driving console, sat an ominous looking stereo system. One thing that really got me about the car was how much space there was, the seats were almost like armchairs, if you wanted to, you could really stretch out.

A light flicked on, the back door opened and Hayley quietly slipped in behind me.

I looked in the internal mirror and saw her full red lips smiling back.

"Where are you taking me then, Skinner?" The red lips asked.

I laughed nervously, "Er yeah I er… Can be your chauffeur."

Hayley snorted and looked out of the window. Quickly say something, I thought, then the driver's door opened, and whatever witty comment I didn't have coming was silenced.

Alan tapped my leg. "Oi Skinner don't get too comfortable in there, mate," he said, grinning.

Dave said, "Come on then, let's go for a spin." Dying to get it out onto the road.

I hopped out, went around to the shotgun seat, while Dave got in, turned over the engine, and it purred into life, rumbling menacingly.

"Oi Hayley get out girl come on mooooooove…" Dave quietly Alan-ed, to his sister in the back, who threw her head back laughing, reaching for the door, doing what she was told.

Alan and Hayley waved us off as we pulled away from the forecourt of the all-night garage, and we headed off down the A10 towards Ware.

Dave drove us past the Sow and Pigs pub, past the bus stop where I had spent so much time waiting, hoping it wouldn't come, so I wouldn't have to go to school, then once we hit the open road that lay between Thundridge and Ware, he stamped on the accelerator and the car almost took off; the power coming from the 1600cc engine was endless.

"Whoa bloody hell!!" I said, as I was pushed back into my seat.

"Yeah, it's amazing, isn't it," said Dave, shifting forward in his seat.

"It's almost like G force," I said.

Dave laughed and pulled a tape from the glove compartment, dexterously pushed it into the stereo system, turning it right up.

"Listen to this Skin, you won't believe it."

G.B.H.'s 'Race against Time' blasted out from the speakers behind us on the back window ledge, filling the car with a wall of Brummie guitars. I sat back, spun down the window, nodding along to Col singing about his race against time, feeling the cool night air rushing onto my face, taking one deep breath after another. A feeling of peace washed over me, it felt good, it felt right, I felt alive, I looked to Dave, he was feeling it too, nodding along, beaming, absolutely delighted with his new acquisition. I thought this is brilliant, in fact, no it's better than brilliant, we are the dog's bollocks in this.

A couple of circuits of the small town of Ware, and we cruised back along the high street to the sounds of G.B.H.'s 'Sick Boy' booming from the stereo, where I saw a punk girl on the near side of the road, next to the thief's paradise Boots, walking away from us.

Punk girls were a rare site in Ware after 1978, even the soft core Siouxsie one's like this one, with her spiked black hair, black leather jacket and thigh high boots were hardly seen any more.

"Oh what, look at that, it's a punk girl, you seen her before?" I exclaimed.

Dave laughed, "What? You're joking, aren't you?"

"No, what? You know her?"

"Yeah and so do you, it's Cerys, you know, your old girlfriend, bloody hell mate get a grip."

"Nah, surely not," I said, dubiously.

"Cerys wasn't into punk when I went out with her, she was a cosmic, mate."

"Cosmics, yeah I remember them," said Dave and he sang in the voice of a bell end, "I've been working my way back to you, babe, with a happiness inside."

I snorted, gave him a sideways look and we both creased up.

"I remember that she used to sing it all the time to wind me up, it did too, what a load of shit that was."

Dave nodded, eyes on the road ahead. "I bet, that was years ago, people change," he said, wisely.

"Yeah, it certainly looks like it, Dave pull over man, let's say hello."

Dave hit the horn, causing her to jump - she must have been miles away.

"Whoops!" He said, pulling a grimace onto his face.

Dave pulled up next to her, she looked suspiciously at this unknown car, our silhouettes and then back at the car again like she was thinking 'oh here we go again'.

"You alright Cerys? Long time no see," I said, sticking my head out of the window.

She smiled self-consciously, "Oh hi, Skinner."

I couldn't resist it, "I thought you said you were going to be a cosmic forever?"

Cerys gave me a confused look. "Aw yeah, my taste in music's changed a bit since then," she laughed, catching on.

"It must have," I said, exaggeratedly checking out her clothes for effect.

Cerys looked around me, shining her emerald, green eyes on Dave, "I heard you were getting a new car, Dave, it's lovely, isn't it?"

"Cheers." Dave said, modestly.

"I wonder by any chance if it was Diane who told you that?" He added, smiling broadly.

She giggled, "How did you guess?"

"Hmm, call it intuition."

Cerys smiled, "I was supposed to be meeting her in the pub, well about an hour ago but the sodding buses…" And shrugged her shoulders.

"Oh right, that's where we were going, wasn't it Skin?" Dave lied.

"Er yeah, that's exactly where we were going, weren't we Dave?"

"So, do you want a lift them?" Dave asked.

"Yeah, ta."

Cerys opened the sleek silver door and placed one high black leather booted leg into the car, Dave glanced over at me, nodding, as if to say, go for it Skinner my old son, I smiled gratefully back.

A while later, after dropping Cerys off, so she could get ready and parking the 1600e safety back under the car port back at Dave's place, we entered our part of The Anchor.

A huge cheer erupted as we entered, it was heaving for a Tuesday night, everyone was in. Cerys' older brother Simon 'Taddy' Ash, Craig, Julie Goddsave, Clare Jonas, Alison Jonas, Ronnie O'Keefe, Phil Buttercroft, Glyn, David 'Sid' Crane, Lee and his skin girl girlfriend Karen, Tracey 'Down in One' Downey, her mate Lucy 'Flat' Chesterman, even Simmy and Macc had left the comfort of the snugs in the main bar to put an appearance in.

Dave and me quickly grabbed four chairs and set the drinks up, talking to the others, while we waited for the girls to arrive.

I had known Cerys Ash and Diane Hyde since The Junior Metal Institution. Dave, me, Christopher 'ears pinned back, hmm… technical Patterson' used to hang around with her older brother Taddy during play time.

One day while we were playing football, he pointed out his little sister Cerys on the climbing frame, who gawked back at her older brother Simon with his best mate, Skinner.

Immediately I noticed her long black hair and dark skin, "Simon, your sister looks like a witch."

"She is a witch," he stated in no uncertain terms.

A few years later, a car park at the back of her house, we named the square, became a regular meeting place for the younger teens in the village, so we saw each other all the time and soon started dating, we were only little kids, though.

Once I start hanging out with Pete as part of the 'S.P.E.N.D' mob, I stopped hanging out in the square and we sort of fizzled out.

One of my first kisses had been with Cerys' best mate Diane Hyde, it had happened on the waste ground out the back of her house when I was around ten years old, I liked her a lot, but as we had grown up, I found I just couldn't click with her, she seemed to live in a world of forced joviality, her over enthusiasm about everything used to do my head in. I thought she would have made a great kids TV presenter with all her energy.

Diane was an amazing looking girl, whose Betty Davis eyes drew the blokes in from miles away like tractor beams, so I doubt my lack of

55

interest bothered her too much. Diane loved attention and had gone out with most of the lads in the village, some lasting a couple of weeks, others a lot longer; at one time some people thought Craig and Diane might get married one day. I wasn't one of them; Craig's idea of a good time was sitting in The Anchor all night getting pissed up; Diane was a lot more ambitious than that, she was going places.

Dave and me sunk a couple of pints each, and then the girls showed up.

Diane sat down and grabbed Dave's arm, squeezing it excitedly, gushing, "Where's your car? I want to see it; it sounds amazing, Dave."

Dave smiled, "Sorry Diane, I've left it at home, I'm having a few drinks tonight."

"Yes, yes that's very grown up of you, very mature well done," she said, smoothing her tight yellow skirt down.

"And how are you, Skinner?" She said, turning her Betty Davis eyes on me.

"Yeah, good Diane, cheers."

"And how's the band, are you a pop star yet?"

I laughed, "Nah not yet, we had a…"

"Sorry," she said, interrupting, holding her hand up, looking over my head,

"Hi Simmy, hi Macc, I hope you're not going to get too drunk tonight," she chimed, waving exaggeratedly in their direction.

Simmy and Macc sat bolt upright in their chairs, pushing their chests out, picking up their drinks toasting her, she shrieked with laughter.

"Cheer's boys, now where were we, oh yes, Skinner the band?"

"So, are you working now?" I asked Cerys.

Cerys took a sip of her pernod and black, before casually replacing it on the table, "I'm working at Van Hage's Garden centre... Unfortunately."

I smiled, "I know that place, they've got all those wild budgies flying about."

Cerys sadly shook her head, "No, not any more they don't, they had some trouble with sparrowhawks."

"What's that got to do with budgies, it's the sparrows that should be worried," I laughed at my amazing joke.

She snorted, "You haven't changed a bit."

I Frank Carson-ed, "It's the way I tell them."

"Hmm it is, anyway, I don't think I'm going to be there much longer."

"Why what happened?" I said, extremely maturely, still laughing internally at my joke.

Cerys eyed me carefully, knowing I was still thinking about my joke, "Well, it's a bit embarrassing… I was working on one of the tills and well, someone I fancy came in with his parents and I must have got confused because when we cashed up later, we were fifty-seven pence short."

"Bloody hell, fifty-seven pence, that buys you nothing in that place."

"Yeah, it is a bit like that. Anyway, I got taken into the manager's office and given a right
rollicking. I was told that 'I'd never be anything in my life'."

I sniggered, "What… Over fifty-seven pence? Who's the manager? Fagan, that old geezer off Oliver Twist?"

"I know, it's ridiculous, isn't it? I wouldn't have minded so much, but it was Mrs. Van Hage who said it."

"Yeah, it's time to leave, Cerys, that's out of order."

Cerys nodded her head firmly like I had helped her make up her mind.

I took a sip of the sweet snakebite,

"I went to school with her son, Frances van Hage, the boy who could fly."

"I don't get it," she said, picking up her drink.

"Frances Van Ears."

She giggled, "Aw… That's mean."

Dave came in on the side and agreed, "That's a little bit harsh, isn't it?"

"Harsh realities of life, my friend," I said.

"Come on, they're not that bad," said Cerys.

"Oh what? They are, one of my mates at school reckoned that if he faced north, he could pick up radio Moscow."

Diane, Cerys and Dave dissolved into fits of laughter.

"Hey, maybe there's some way to electrify his ears, then he can stand out near the budgie cages and electrocute any stray sparrowhawks," I said, feeling a surge of alcohol inside me taking over.

Dave and Diane cracked up laughing all over again, Cerys smiled politely, shook her head, asked if anyone wanted another drink, and we all replied in the affirmative.

A few too many drinks later, when last orders came, we grabbed a couple more drinks, downed them quickly, walked out of the warmth of the pub into the cool fresh air of night and stood under the yellow spotlight lights of The Anchor pub sign.

"OK Skin, I'm going to walk Diane home, I'll meet you by the bridge," Dave said, with a tiny nod of encouragement.

"I'll walk you home then, Cerys," I stated, almost like a question.

"OK," she said, coyly.

Cerys and me didn't stop talking all the way back to her house, when we got to her front gate, I drunkenly leant on it, and it fell inwards, away from me, so I quickly righted myself.

"It's been really nice catching up with you, can I see you again?" I asked, hoping she hadn't noticed.

Cerys smiled broadly through the darkness; she'd noticed alright, "I'd like that, it's been fun."

"It would be even better if I could stay upright," I said, looking accusingly at the gate.

Cerys smiled, leant forwards and planted a sweet kiss on my cheek.

"See ya."

"Yeah, see you, Cerys."

Cerys hurried down the garden path, stopped at her front door, turned, smiled, gave me a huge wave and then closed it gently behind her.

I was on top of the world, as I walked back up her street, even though I'd nearly flattened her mums winter bedding. I couldn't stop smiling, Cerys and me had always got on, and now she was into punk. It was a match made in 'heathen', I thought, a punk rocker girlfriend would be great, someone who liked the same music, saw the world the way I did. Now my old girlfriend, someone I knew to be a laugh and a good person, was a punk; it couldn't have been better.

On the main road, I saw Dave silhouetted against a background of orange light, emitting from the road works on the bridge opposite The Anchor.

"What happened then?" He said, as I got close.

I said, "A kiss." Puckering up.

Dave put his fist up like he had just scored the winning goal in a tight 3-2 match,

"Yeeees, nice one Skinner nice one son, nice one Skinner, let's have another one."

Dave and me drunkenly jumped up and down celebrating, both laughing our heads off.

"I knew you'd be alright; romance is in the air?" Dave said, confidently.

"Oh what, careful that sounds a bit Mills and Boon mate," I laughed.

"No not at all, Hayley's in to all that astrology stuff, you know the movement of planets affecting our lives and all that, she reckoned Venus is rising, so it's a good time for a new relationship."

"You sure she said, 'Venus' man, something was definitely rising tonight," I quipped.

Dave cracked up, "No look up there look, that bright star in the north, that's Venus," he said pointing.

61

I squinted my eyes up, "I can't see a thing Dave, those fucking traffic lights, hold up, I'll sort this out."

I strode over to the road works, picked up one of the concrete bottomed lamps, lobbed it over the side of the bridge, watching it disappear into the darkness.

SPLASH

I recoiled from the edge as the water came up high enough to touch the bottom of the bridge, the sound echoing off underneath it. Dave appeared next to me, lugging another one, hoisted it high above his head, launched it into the gloom, and we waited, 3, 2, 1.

"Nice one, Dave, I want to see Venus rinsing."

SPLASH… another mini tsunami of water came up from the depths.

"Rising yet, Skin?"

SPLASH

"Oh OK, so Venus is rising, and these traffic lights are sinking."

SPLASH

Dave cracked up

SPLASH

"I bet the old bloke on The Sky at Night Patrick Moore has never had to do this to see Venus," said Dave, sending me into fits of laughter.

SPLASH

SPLASH

Once we had chucked all of them in, tired, drunk, needing a rest after our exertions, we looked over the edge, to take in our handy work.

An incredible sight met our eyes, we couldn't believe it, all the traffic lights now submerged deep at the bottom of the river were still working; miraculously flashing back up at us.

Orange on. Orange off. Orange on. Orange off.

Dave and me were mesmerized by the hypnotic orange lights pulsing out of the gloom at the bottom of the river, it was one of the best light shows I had ever seen, it was free too.

One moment chaotic, random, the next rhythmic, oscillating, on, off, on, off, pulsing like disco lights, then slowly rescinding, going out of time to become chaos again.

It was like a celestial body had fallen from the sky, crash-landed in the river rib, and was now sending out a distress message; Dave and me were powerless to resist its call.

A police bike sped past us on the bridge, bringing an end to our extra-terrestrial viewing.

I said, "Oh fucking hell," under my breath.

Dave and me looked at each other and nodded, deciding without

63

words, that it was time to get the hell out of there, so we slunk off, and just to be on the safe side we took the back route up Ermine Street away from the main road and any more bacon on speeding bikes.

I said, "So where's Venus then, Dave?" As we passed Tarnia Gordon's house.

Dave looked up into the jewel encrusted sky, turned to the north.

"It's that one there, mate," pointing at the glinting orb.

"Oh yeah, I see, beautiful, maaan…" I said, putting a bit of sarcasm into it, "Nah… it's been good seeing Cerys again, I hope Hayley's right."

Chapter 5

Cannon Fodder

One fine sunny day, Andy, Whiff and me were sitting in The Anchor, three pints lined up in front of us, when Dave came in with a broad smile on his face, telling us that he had got us a gig at Thundridge Youth Club. Bob, one of the youth leaders, was not only a decent bloke, he was also Dave's uncle too, so I wasn't surprised; it was a shoe in really.

"Nice one Dave," I said, buying him a pint in recognition for his services to the band, lining it up with the rest.

Dave took a huge draft, wiped the froth from his chin and burped extravagantly, "We need to take the swearing down, though, Bob said he was worried about what some parents might say."

"Oh what, no, really? That's all part of who we are," I protested.

Dave nodded, understanding how we all felt, "Yeah… I know Skin, I kind of promised him though…"

I asked everyone else what they thought, we soon agreed that the odd 'fuck' here and there would probably be OK; it probably wouldn't be heard over the mayhem we created anyway. 'Christ Fuckers' one of the favourite tracks, the one we all really wanted to play had over twenty fucks in it, so instead of dropping it altogether we decided to cut the multiple fucks from the chorus, and leave the rest up to Andy and how he felt on the day to self-censor himself.

Whiff got another round in, we sat back, sipping our snakebites talking excitedly about the gig, how it would be different from

Richard Hole and how we could make it better. One thing we kept coming back to, was that this wasn't going to be a normal kind of gig for us, not only would we be playing in front of a bunch of little kids, we would also be playing in front of my mates who listened to Madness, The Specials and apart from hearing the odd test tape track they had never heard our brand of punk before. I thought that we would probably blow their fucking heads off after listening to all that bullshit, still I wanted them to like us, so we needed to find a solution that would work for both us and them.

In the end, Whiff suggested we should do a showcase gig, only playing the first three tracks of our set, which I thought was a great idea and after kicking it around for a while we all agreed, that's what we would do. It would be Virus V1's version of Thatcher's, short, sharp, shock.

A couple of pints later, I was beginning to feel the effects of the alcohol, when Danny entered the pub looking pleased with himself, "Oi, Skinner have you heard?"

"What, that you're a knob end?" I said.

Danny laughed, "No, we are going to get our own village copper."

A chorus of laughter echoed around the bar as we fell about laughing at the prospect of having our own personal pet plod in the village.

"Here comes the policeman, the big friendly policeman, PC McGarry number 452," sang Andy, showing us he had been watching TV with his little brothers again.

Danny told us, Hertfordshire Constabulary were fed up with the amount of vandalism in the village, and they were going to put a stop to it, by sending in a beat cop to keep an eye on us, which had us creasing up all over again.

"It's a proud moment in the history of the village," I said, standing up, raising my glass aloft.

Andy whiff and Dave joined me, toasting the incoming Angeln saddleback.

"I wonder who they are sending? Is it Steve McGarrett from Hawaii 5-0?" I asked.

"Thundridge 5-0," Andy corrected.

Whiff grinned, "I hope it's Sabrina from Charlie's Angels."

Dave snorted, "Sabrina? What!!! You could have chosen Farrah Fawcett or Jaclyn Smith, and you chose Sabrina."

I laughed, "He'd probably end up with Charlie."

Whiff looked hurt, "Oi… piss off, I like Sabrina."

Dave scrutinized him curiously for a while. "Oddball," he concluded.

"No, it's Cannon, his name is PC Cannon," said Danny.

"What like Private Investigator Frank Cannon, that fat bastard on the TV? Fuck off," I told him.

Danny laughed, "No, it is… He's coming to the youth club next week to introduce himself."

Once we had wiped the tears of laughter from our stinging eyes, we quickly agreed that it was unmissable, whatever happened, fire, earthquake, flood, even if Whiff had a date with Sabrina from Charlie's Angels, we would all be there.

*

Thundridge youth club had been set up by Bob Williams and Colin Hill to stop the trouble in the village, it worked in as much that kids stopped causing trouble in the village on Thursday nights when it was open, but on the other six nights as the boredom took hold, it was business as usual. I wasn't into it, after my first visit, as quite a few of the younger kids used to go. Also, the music being played on the donated stereo system was absolute shit, sometimes it was so bad, it felt like radio one DJ Simon Bates had got himself a residency at Thundridge Village Hall.

Whiff started going out with a girl called Paula Gates, who looked great, liked a laugh and loved going to the youth club, so with Whiff there every Thursday night, I couldn't not go. I didn't know Paula very well; I knew her mum though, she had left an indelible image on my mind, an image that had given me a clue to what my future teenage interests would be, when she was working as a dinner lady at The Junior Mental institution. Mrs. Gates was a pleasant, friendly, middle-aged woman, who always had a smile for you, no matter how busy she was, unlike her co-worker Mrs. Sampson, The Soup Dragon, whose face was perpetually set to miserable.

I was nine years old; a table monitor, Mrs. Gates, was taking the order for my table when she inadvertently dropped a spoon. It clattered to the floor and as she leant forward to retrieve it, she revealed her cavernous cleavage to me. Instantly something stirred in my loins, I had never felt that before, a nice warm feeling spread

68

around my body, a longing, an excitement, a craving that begun its journey in between my legs, ending its journey up in my head; my face turned puce. I tried to look away, it was impossible, I became lost in her mammoth bosom, she noticed, she smiled at the red-faced little kid, who didn't know where to look now, and completed the order.

Mrs. Gates smiled again at the confused little kid, we all said thank you, and she pushed her trolley onto the next table, and my first, brief, if extremely informative sex education lesson was over.

On the night of PC Cannon's introduction, I was sitting, drinking a can of Coke with Ronnie, looking over at Paula talking to Dave and Andy thinking about her mum again, when Whiff came in through the double doors, saw me and pulled The Exploited's new album 'Troops for Tomorrow' from a yellow Tracks bag, waving at me, grinning like a mad bastard.

"Skin you've got to hear this, Big John's guitar sound is fucking brilliant, I'm putting this on."

"You reckon? Good luck with that mate," I said looking over at the club's stereo system

Ian Simms, Simmy's little brother, was doing his usual 'DJ' stint.

"I'm not backing down this time I tell you, it's fucking going on," said Whiff, his eyes fixed on DJ Ian.

Ian Simms, wore milk bottle glasses, had wild ginger hair and was about five years younger than me. He lived in a dilapidated house at the top of my road with his three sisters, two brothers, eight cats, six dogs and more rabbits than in Mr. McGregor's back garden. On most days, Ian acted like the rest of us kids in the village, but now and again, if he was having a bad day, his behaviour would lead you to believe there might be something wrong with him; a few of the older and nastier people in the village called him the village idiot.

I watched in trepidation as Whiff approached him.

"You alright, Ian, can you put this on?" Whiff asked.

Ian looked up irritably from the revolving record deck and gave the record a cursory glance.

"No," Ian replied, as though he was addressing a particularly bothersome child.

"Look, come on, stop hogging it, let someone else have a go."

Ian boggled at him through thick glass, "I'm a DJ, and you're not, so go away."

Whiff looked over, shook his head and defeatedly walked back as Culture club's 'Karma Chameleon' came on for the third time that evening.

"What a prat," muttered Whiff, sitting down hard.

"I'm putting my record on, I'm telling you," he said, determinedly.

"Fucking hope so, mate, I can't handle another bout of Culture Club's 'Stoma Comedian'."

Whiff and me sat back, enduring another four or five hits from the pop picker, hoping to get a chance to change the bloody record, then hallelujah, our chance came.

Ian left the decks unattended to go to the toilet, leaving the bilge that is Black Lace 'Superman' spinning on the turntable.

"OK, watch this," said Whiff, seizing the moment.

Whiff ran over to the unattended deck, quickly queued up the 'Troops of Tomorrow' album and Big John's guitar blasted out into the hall, at the start of 'U.K. 82', sending Ian running back from the toilets, still doing his flies up, his eyes bugging out, pointing at Whiff.

"Oi you! Did you touch my records?"

Whiff looked at him evenly, "Yeah."

"That's theft, that is," Ian bellowed.

Whiff laughed, "What? No, it isn't"

"I'm calling the coppers!"

Whiff, finally losing it, said, "Ah, do what you fucking like, you idiot."

Ian boggled at him, almost frothing at the mouth, "I'm going to tell Bob, and then he's going to call the coppers, you'll be in trouble then."

Ian rushed off cornering Bob and Colin Hill who were watching Taddy and Craig play pool on the club's table as 'Troops of Tomorrow' blasted out through the youth club. I was just marvelling

71

at the sound that Big John had got on his guitar, as Whiff had told me I would, when our new village policeman, PC Cannon, shouldered his way in through the double doors.

Ian leapt up, bounded over to Whiff, "See this copper? This copper's come for you; you're going to jail."

Ian belted over to his saviour, like his life depended on it, and began gesticulating wildly, pointing at us, the record thieves. PC Cannon frowned, totally bewildered, shook his head dismissively at Ian, who just gesticulated even more. Ian had caught us in the act, the weight of law was on his side, the criminals were not only bang to rights, they were sitting on the other side of the hall in fits of laughter.

A couple of minutes passed with PC Cannon shaking his head, left, right, left, right, like a confused nodding dog, and Ian nodding his head up, down, up, down like an unconfused nodding dog.

I snorted, "Oh well, he definitely isn't Private Investigator Frank Cannon from the TV, is he? … He got through the double doors ok."

"I don't know, still could be him, they say that going on TV puts ten pounds on you," said Dave, coming over to join in the merriment.

"Yeah, ten pounds maybe, it would be ten stone in this case, Frank Cannon's a proper fat bastard, he's got a wide vehicle badge on his car and his arse."

"He looks more like PC Mc Gary 492," Andy added, and burst into song, "Here comes the Policeman, the big friendly Policeman, PC McGarry No. 452. Lost a key, cat up a tree, lost a shoe? Then get a policeman, a friendly policeman. PC McGarry No. 452…"

Dave repeated, "Lost a shoe?" Putting his head in hands.

I creased up, "I think he looks more like Dixon of Dock Green...
Or should I say, Dickhead of Dock Green," correcting myself.

"He's still better looking than Sabrina though," said Dave, eying
Whiff, looking for a rise.

"Oi piss off Sabrina's well horny," said Whiff, rising.

Dave grinned at Andy and me, "Oddball."

PC Cannon eventually fended off Ian; the first kid he had spoken to
in the village, which had clearly unnerved him, and turned his
attention to the club's two youth leaders, Bob and Colin. PC Cannon
gave them an ingratiating smile, a firm handshake and pleasantries
over with, they took him for a tour of the club. To the pool table,
the dart board, and the table football, making sure to steer him well
clear of the stereo system as DJ Ian was back in residency and not
only that, he was still insisting that arrests should be made.

Bob and Colin introduced him to some of the more law-abiding
kids, while he stood back like he was Napoleon in a tit head helmet
inspecting the troops before the battle of Austerlitz. It wasn't going
well, monosyllabic replies, snorts and surly sour faces were all they
were getting for their trouble, so Bob and Colin cut his inspection
short, calling for everyone to be quiet. PC Cannon wanted to address
us all on a very important matter.

A cold silence settled over the hall, PC Cannon bombastically
marched away from Bob and Colin onto a small staircase and up
onto the stage, where he stopped centre stage. Laurel and Hardy's

73

theme tune whistled tunefully out from where Craig and Taddy were standing, producing a chorus of laughs, even Bob and Colin were grinning. PC Cannon cleared his throat, and we all fell silent again, waiting for the next chapter in our village's history to begin, waiting for the bullshit, waiting for the hilarity.

"Hello, my name is PC Cannon, and I am now your village policeman. You're going to be seeing a lot of me around the village, so if you need any help, all you need to do is ask."

BRRRRRRAAAAAAAAAPPPPPP!

A huge fart emanated from where Taddy and Craig were standing.

"Er, you dirty git," said Craig, moving away from his smelly mate.

"I… I… Yes, yes, ahem, now I don't want to be here, and I'm sure you don't want me to be here either," said PC Cannon.

"No, we don't," stated Lucy Flat Chesterman, evenly.

"Yes well, ahem, hem, hem… well I'm only here because there's been a lot of trouble in this lovely village, we've had a lot of complaints from law-abiding citizens, who quite frankly have had enough of it and quite rightly so, that's why I'm here."

Bob stood up and looked at us, "OK thank you very much PC C…"

"Now I don't think this is a bad village, not a bad village at all, far from it. I think most of you are decent and well-behaved, but unfortunately there are some amongst you, a few individuals, ahem…" he said, his eyes fixing on Dave and me.

Whiff grinned; Andy gave me a nudge; I looked back with a sweet 'what me' face.

PC Cannon droned on, "…who are ruining it for everyone else, especially the young ones, it's not fair on them or anyone, so if anyone has any information about these troublemakers you can speak to me or one of the youth leaders in complete confidence, so please don't hesitate, I'm here to help you, and together we'll stop these hooligans and make Thundridge the village it once was, thank you, ahem…"

PC Cannon stood back, hands on hips, puffing himself up like he had just addressed the United Nations, looking around at us like he was expecting a round of applause.

Instead, a wall of silence greeted him, never before have I seen so much hatred focused on one area. Craig, Taddy, Mal 'À La Tete' Ferguson, Lee and Glyn were standing arms crossed looking defiant, behind them Ronnie, Danny, Phil, Martin 'Coops' Cooper, 'Brother' Vincent Macc and Russ Banks were all leaning in, dossing the twat out, even the girls looked angry. Julie, Karen, Tracy, Sally, Rachel could hardly contain their rage and Lucy flat Chesterman, well she viewed him, like he had just pissed all over her Toyah collection.

In the past we were just a group of kids messing about in the village, having a laugh, trying to break the boredom. Now that we had our own pet policeman, Pig Man Cannon as he had been christened, it would be so much better, as it would be more of a challenge and involve more danger, so it would be double the laugh, in fact it would be irresistible.

A week of insurrection began. Everyone was at it.

The local telephone box had all its windows smashed, the directory ripped to shreds, left to blow down Ermine Street; Cannon was called.

A group of fishermen were pelted with overripe plums as they quietly fished the river rib; Cannon was called.

An old couple had been startled while they peacefully played a game of chess in their front room when someone smudged their arse onto their front window, mooning them; Cannon was called.

French foreign exchange students had their bright cagoule jackets stolen, while they were brass rubbing at All Saints and Hallows church, known locally as the old church; Cannon was called.

Cars had been damaged after someone had lost control while doing doughnuts in the square; Cannon was called.

A school coach had its tyres slashed as it waited at the bus stop; Cannon was called.

Customers at the all-night garage on the A10 had been showered with stones while they filled up their cars; Cannon was called.

A bounty of cigarettes, bacci pouches and porn mags had been stolen from the local shop by persons unknown, kicking in the back doors; Cannon was called.

On the Friday night of PC Cannon's first week as our village policeman, all the road signs along the A10 in the village mysteriously vanished; Cannon was called.

People in the village were beginning to notice how much worse it had become since PC Cannon had showed up, which in turn made him even more determined to make it stop. If he wasn't patrolling in his light blue panda car, he would put on his tit head helmet and go out on the beat, talk to people, see what he could find out, slyly creeping around the younger kids in a futile attempt to garner information, which was never forthcoming.

A few days after Danny's now notorious theft of the road signs, I was hanging around with Cerys outside her house with her, Dave, Tom 'Laurel' Hardy, Glyn, Lee, Ronnie and some of their little brothers and sisters when we were disturbed by the sight of PC Cannon's light blue panda car crawling up the street towards us.

"Oink, oink, Cannon fodder approaching," I said, out the corner of my mouth.

PC Cannon cruised past, his head flipping, left, right, left right, rubbernecking us suspiciously, like we were the UK's most wanted. Once he had patrolled the square, finding it clean, and crime free, he came back up the hill, parking up at the top, next to a row of cars.

Dave eyed up the little panda car, "Check this out. I'm going to let the handbrake off!"

"No, Dave!" Cerys said.

"Nah Dave, don't do it mate," I said, backing her up.

"Keep the little bacon butty talking," he said coolly, walking down towards the square.

Once he got to the bottom of the row of cars, he glanced back up at Cannon who was putting his hat on, walking towards Cerys and me.

A wankers sign to Cannon and Dave disappeared behind the cars.

I stifled a laugh. "You alright officer?" I said, as PC Cannon approached us.

"Skinner, isn't it?" He enquired.

"Yeah, what can we do you for officer?" I said, my voice all sweetness and light.

"Oink, Oink, Can, Can Feather," said Ronnie's baby sister Jennifer, squealing with delight.

PC Cannon stopped in his tracks and stared down at baby Jennifer quizzically, the penny dropped, his lip curled up like a snake in a basket, "I'll tell you what you can do for me, you can tell me what happened to those road signs."

I shook my head, "I don't know what you're going on about, mate."

"I tell you what I'm going on about, shall I? Ahem… I'm going on about saving people's lives; road signs are there for a reason. Hem, hem… it could be your Mum and Dad that get hurt!" His voice rising in volume and righteousness.

"Or yours or yours or yours or yours," he said, pointing his fingers around like a gun.

"Oink, fodder, can oink," said Jennifer, running to Ronnie, who swept her up into his arms. "Shhhhhh! No more now, Jen Jen," he cooed.

I swivelled my eyes away from the Tamworth to the row of parked cars, to see how Dave was doing. On his hands and knees, slowly but surely, he was getting closer, sneaking along the back of the row of cars, now and again his head popping up, face becoming more manic as he got ever nearer to his prey, the little blue panda.

Dave, you're a mad bastard, I thought, doing everything I could to stop myself laughing.

I sneered at Cannon, knowing justice was coming, "OK mate, if I see any sign of the signs, I'll give you a sign, I'll sign off for now."

Cerys almost stifled a laugh, Cannon spun on her, visibly shaking with anger.

"Oh, very good, well done, now you listen to me, ahem… I'm not your mate and believe me, people will be arrested over this and the next sign they'll be seeing is ahem, hem, hem… H.M.P. Wormwood scrubs, make no mistake."

"Can, nan, oink, oink, oink, fodder," Jennifer squealed with joy.

On the other side of the road, the little panda's driver side door slowly opened, Dave's grinning head popped up, down, up, down, over the dashboard grinning in our direction. He leant forward, reaching for the handbrake, the suspension gave an audible creak and some of the younger kids looked over towards the police car, wondering what the noise was.

Cannon followed their gaze, Dave saw the game was up, pushed the door to, stood up and walked over the road with a big shit-eating grin on his face.

"Hello matey, you alright, are you mate? I like your motor, lovely seats in there, are they leather?" He said, grinning at the completely confused Cannon.

"Hello, where did you come from....? Ahem... you er..."

Cannon stood for a moment, trying to digest this new development, then it dawned on him.

"You wait here," he commanded, pointing at Dave, before rushing over to his little panda.

PC Cannon circled the car a couple of times, he checked the tyres, he bent down to inspect the paint work, looked at the mirrors, the lights, then he noticed the driver's door was open.

A baffled look came over his face, he slowly opened it. Closed it again. Opened it. Closed it. Opened it and closed it again, checking to see if it was faulty, then scratched at his small chin as if he was trying to remember if he had closed it properly. Once his inspection was completed, he got back into the little panda, turned the engine over, hammered the accelerator and with one last furious look, he disappeared up the street, leaving us all falling about laughing.

"Can, can, oink, oink gone now," said a smiling Jennifer, twisting her hand in her hair.

Chapter 6

Each Day, In Every Way, I'm Getting Better and Better

Whiff had recorded our first gig, so we went back over it, listening to see how we could improve, even though we thought we had done well without a PA system, we all agreed that we needed to do something to enhance our sound, to make our music and message stronger. I knew a bloke called Doggy, who was interested in sound engineering, might be able to help, so I put it to them, and unanimously, they agreed to give him a try. I didn't bother saying anything to Andy about bouncing the two blokes offstage, as I thought he regretted it as much as I regretted calling the CND a bunch of wankers, and it was hilarious listening back to it; it just added to the chaos.

I had known Dave 'Doggy' Kinnell for a long time, as not only did he live just down the road from me, but we did some time together at the Thundridge Junior Mental Institution. Doggy didn't last long though, a couple of years into his stay, his parents, unhappy with the kind of education he was receiving at 'The Bin', believing that some of 'the rough and tumble' type of kids he mixed with were a bad influence on him, uprooted him, sending him to a private school. Doggy had then vanished off the face of the earth as far as his friends were concerned, buried under a mound of piano and prep, I presumed, that is, until I bumped into him on the way back from the pub one night. Doggy was different, he had changed, gone was the easy-going, fun seeking kid I used to know, he was uptight, cringingly open, behaving like your stereo typical, socially inept, privately educated kid. In fact, I thought he was a bit of a prat; a classic case of what over-pushy parents could have on a sensitive soul. I was about to make my excuses to get away from the wishy-washy twat, when he began reminiscing about the old days in 'The

Bin' and suddenly, miraculously, the real Doggy seemed to switch back on again. Doggy became the funny, easy-going kid I used to know, so when he invited me up to Cambridge to smoke some grass with his university pals, I remembered back to the first time I had smoked grass underneath the viaduct in Hertford, the beauty of the shimmering azure River Lee, the internal warmth that spread throughout my body. I'd agreed, thinking it would be good to give it another go.

A few days later, Doggy drove us up to Cambridge, as we travelled up through the villages of north Hertfordshire and into Cambridgeshire, I began to regret my decision to join him, he had switched off again, reverting to a sort of posh Frank Spencer, who wanted to apologise for his very existence on planet Earth.

Doggy was so down on himself, so open about it, that I sat cringing, shuddering awkwardly, nodding my head at the extremely personal details he was disclosing. I was so uncomfortable with the depth of his psychosis, that I was beginning to understand what it was like to be an over worked, overwhelmed psychiatrist, then when he said. 'Every day in every way I'm getting better and better' quoting the hapless Spencer verbatim, I almost opened the car door and jumped out, hoping to end the misery of it all for the both of us.

Once we had met up with his mates at The Boat Race pub in the city centre, it all changed, I put my suicidal thoughts on hold for a while, I soon found out that not all the students at Cambridge University were Jean-Paul Sartre public-school 'the futility of life' victims like Doggy. One in particular, Paul 'Sulli' Sullivan was not only a Crass and Discharge living punk, he sang in a well-known Cambridge punk band called the Sickos, so after downing a few snakebites, with a locally brewed cider each, we hit it off straight away.

I was on my way down to Dave's, a couple of days before our 'showcase' gig, when I saw the familiar sight of Doggy's bedroom light shining out like a beacon in an otherwise dark, cold, unwelcoming house. Oh well, it's now or never, I thought, so I strolled up his long driveway, past the high swaying pampas grass in his front garden, up into his porch and rang the doorbell.

A while later, I was still standing in the gloom when a light flicked on, dazzling me, the door fell inwards to reveal his mum, Elizabeth, wearing a fixed smile on her face. A fixed smile that became unfixed, dropping horribly at the edges, as she scrutinized me like I had just run over Faustus, the family cat, and chucked his lifeless, bloody corpse into her hallway, whilst grinning like Norman Bates at a taxidermist.

I threw a fixed smile back. "Hi, is Dog… er… Douglas in?"

Elizabeth's face clouded over like another blasted rainy day on Ladies Day at Royal Ascot, she said sombrely, "Oh, hello Michael, I'm sorry I think he's busy… Working." Emphasizing the word working.

"OK, Mrs. Kinnell, thanks, I'll come back later, shall I?"

Elizabeth's head nodded a silent reply, concluding this unwarranted, unwanted, intrusion.

"I was wondering can I leave a message?"

"Yes, yes of course," she said, forgetting to tell him already.

I thought, oh well, not to worry, it's only Thundridge Youth Club. Giving up, I turned to leave, when I heard pounding feet on the stairs.

"It's OK mother, let him in," shouted Doggy.

Elizabeth sighed deeply, sighed again, sighed a third time for luck and receiving none, she relented, moving to one side, letting me pass into the tomb like silence of the house.

I followed Doggy up to his bedroom and saw that it was exactly the same as the last time I had been let into the house, about a year earlier. In one corner there was a small desk piled high with books, above the teetering stacks, an angle poise lamp reached out like a gibbet, bleaching out cold, white light. Doggy pulled an embarrassed smile, quickly closing an exercise book on his desk, like it was porn, and I was his mum catching him out. Once the offending, educational and probably quite informative book was disposed of, he extinguished the gibbet, and we sat down on his bed.

A door slammed downstairs, shaking the floorboards under our feet, reminding me that my presence was surplus to requirements, so I thought I had better get straight to it. I told him about our up-and-coming gig, the music we played, and that we were looking to improve our sound. Doggy nodded confidently, he seemed interested, so I pulled out Whiff's tape of our Richard Hole gig from my leather jacket pocket. He took it, spun it over in his hands, giving a cursory glance, then fed it into his impressive stereo system, cranking the volume right up.

"Oh yes, hold on," said Doggy, as he grabbed socks, shirts, skiddy underwear from his wash basket and began wedging them under the door.

I snorted, "Jesus, it's not that bad, mate."

"Oh no, no, no, I'm sure it's not, I've got a little doobie, do you want some?"

"Yeah of course, if I was your Mum and Dad though, I'd rather the smell of cannabis than your shitty underwear," I said, nodding at his impromptu door stop.

"What do you mean? Oh yes, yes, ha, ha, me too," Doggy said, creasing up self-conscientiously, flourishing the doobie in his hand.

Doggy always seemed to have grass around. I smiled broadly.

"Oh what, nice one!" I said, admiring his handy work.

Doggy threw open the window, letting some cool evening air into the stale room, "We will have to blow the smoke out of here Skinner, you see Mother and Father don't know I smoke it, in fact they don't even know I smoke at all, well I don't smoke normal ones, so they're half right I suppose," he told me, nodding at his own wisdom.

Doggy took a quick puff, blew the white fumes out of the window and passed it to me, and I weaved around him, taking the position at the window.

A couple of minutes into the tape, he said, "Hmmm, I can see what you've done wrong here."

I nodded steadily, "What?"

Doggy waved me away, "Oh, you don't need to worry about that, all you need to know is I'm going to make you sound better than you ever have."

I thought that's a bold claim, it sounds like you know what you are doing, this could work out well for everyone. It'll get Doggy out of the house for a while, get him away from his books, maybe liven the bloke up a bit, and in the process, make us sound a whole lot better.

"OK mate, cheers, if you can do that, that would be brilliant… That sounds great."

Doggy giggled and punned, "Your sound will be great."

I nodded and exhaled a nimbus cloud of smoke out of the window, watching the shadowy, feather like plumes of the pampas grass, waving gently, in his front garden.

"Ah, that's a nice bit of smoke mate, where did you get that? Is it Cambridge grass?" I asked, turning.

"Yeah, as ever, trusty old Cambridge," came the dreamy reply.

I sighed, looking back out into the darkness and saw the white of Elizabeth's face in the light of the study window frowning up at me.

I did a double-take, by take two she had vanished, a door slammed, shaking the house again, then the porch light flashed on, off, on, off, on, off petulantly.

"Oh, fucking hell, your mum just saw me," I said, ducking back inside.

"Ha, ha, hassler," He guffaws.

"No, seriously mate…"

"Douglas…"
"Douglas…"
"DOUGLAS…"
"DOUGLAS…"

All the colour drained from Doggy's face.

I winced, "Oh shit, I told you, mate."

"OK, it's OK. It's OK, I'll be OK, I'll be OK, each day, in every way, I'll be OK," He burbled, trying to convince himself that it would be OK this time.

"You going to be alright, mate?"

"Yes, yes, I told you yes, yes I'll be OK, I think we had better throw the doobie away though," he said, shakily moving his now totally obsolete door stop out of the way, then like a dead man walking, he walked out of his bedroom and downstairs, to face the music.

I thought, waste not, want not, so I pinched the orange ember off the spliff, dropped it out of the window, and stuck the remains into my pocket for later.

In Doggy's absence, I looked around the room again. It was weird to say the least, it was like there were actually two people living here. One was into Pink Floyd, Frank Zappa, Steve Hillage, read Sound Magazine and had a decent array of sound processors. The other one, lived over near the angle poise gibbet, was into Maths,

Chemistry, Physics, Biology, Art History, Shakespeare, Charles Dickens and read the Financial Times; it was like the room had a split personality.

A long while later, a browbeaten Doggy re-emerged, sat down on his bed underneath his 'dark side of the moon' poster, looked down, eyes focused solely on the brown carpet.

"You OK mate, what happened?" I asked.

"I'm sorry Skinner, I said it was your dope," he said, with a torn, anguished looked on his face.

I half-laughed, "Oh what, cheers mate, thanks for that."

"I know, I know, I shouldn't have done it, I'm sorry, I didn't know what else to say," he said, his hand flailing around on his forehead.

I sighed inwardly, feeling sorry for the bloke, so what if they thought it was my dope, when it came down to it, I didn't care, his parents had made up their minds about me a long time ago.

"Ah, don't worry about it mate, just make us sound good at the gig yeah?" I said, trying to lighten his load.

"Yes, I will, I will, cheers Skinner, you've saved my bacon."

I laughed, "Nah… It's fine mate, they'll just think I'm still a 'rough and tumble' type of kid."

"Oh, yes 'a rough and tumble kid', I remember that," nodding his head vigorously, creasing up laughing.

"OK look, I better go now… before you drop me in it anymore."

"I'm so sorry, I really am."

I held up my hand for him to stop, "I'll see you at the pavilion Friday night mate."

"OK, I can't wait," he said and cautiously showed me out of the house, furtively looking out for mother, hoping she would stay in the lounge.

*

I warned everyone what Doggy was like, while we were setting up at the pavilion. I don't think Dave and Whiff believed a word of it, in this day and age it just didn't seem possible to them. Andy did though, as like me, he had met these types of kids at Richard Hole on a daily basis, their ongoing psychosis, a by-product of the school's obsession with results and attainment.

Doggy was late, which pissed us off. All of us being conscious of the fact that we weren't supposed to practice on a Friday night, we were all itching to go when he finally walked in.

I introduced him to everyone, introductions over, instead of setting up his gear, getting down to business, he went into a long diatribe about the problems he was having with someone we neither knew, nor cared about and for some reason, he had a cockney accent now.

Doggy was having a great time, he was completely unaware of how ridiculous his Arthur Daley approximation of the cockney brogue sounded or how pissed off we all were getting, waiting to get started, but he just blathered on and on regardless.

"OK, Dave… Look, shall we get on now?" I said, eventually.

"Yes, yes of course," he apologised profusely in a Cambridge accent, then went straight down the M11 to the Mile End Road with, "Yeah, yeah, yeah, of course mate."

I ran my hand back through my ginger and brown spikes and looked at everyone else's semi-amused, mystified faces, which all seemed to be asking the same question - is this your mate, Skinner?

"OK, so where's your gear then?"

"I haven't brought it with me, I thought it might get damaged."

Silence resonated around the pavilion; I began to wonder who was going to start taking the piss out of him first. My money was on Whiff as ever.

"Oh right, er… We'll just play a couple of tracks, see what you think, OK?"

"Yeah, alwight mate."

Dave launched into the intro of V1 Bomb hammering the snare into submission, I hit the dampened guitar riff, Dave ran the sticks across the kit, we all came in, we were off, up and running, while Doggy sat back, nodding his head, figuring out what was required.

On the second verse of V1 Bomb, Doggy stood up and put his hand up in the air.

"Yeah, yeah, yeah, that's great, great, great. I know just what we need to do," he said, like he was addressing the chorus line at the Hackney Empire.

"I don't," Andy said, semi-jokingly.

"I do," Doggy said, looking at Andy like he was a bit slow.

"I'm gonna make you sound better than you ever 'ave," gawd blimey-ed Doggy.

Andy scratched his head puzzled, "OK, so what are you going to do?"

Doggy straighten up, meeting the challenge, "Ah…don't worry about it mate, I've done this all before. I ain't trying to show off or nothing, but I've been with bigger bands than you lot, I can tell ya, tell ya that for nuthink."

Andy stepped towards him; I quickly got up, smiling, gave him an 'it's not worth it' look.

"OK, so you've got what you need then?" I asked, keeping my voice level, hoping Andy would stop dossing him out.

"I was in a band called Charlotte's Party, we were on Anglia News one night, and we made it to national battle of the bands final in London, it was… we went to Wembley, where the footy is and……we were contenders……a good experience……" on and on he went, and as he droned on, his fake cockney accent slowly disappeared, along with our patience.

I don't know why I agreed to it but when we left the pavilion, Doggy came with us, we did a quick lap of the village, ending up back at Dave's house, where we found Ann busy in the kitchen cleaning up and setting the places out for the next morning's breakfast.

"Hello, what are you reprobates up to?" She asked, with her usual welcoming smile.

"We've come to rob this house," said a grinning Dave to his mum, who burst into laughter.

In true Ann spirit, even though she had a lot on, she offered us all a cup of tea, while she was faffing, getting it together, pulling the chocolate biscuits out for the always hungry teenagers, she asked Doggy if he would like sugar in his tea.

Even though he'd been Whitechapel Road born and bred most of the evening, he Windsor Castle-ed, "Oh yes please, that would be lovely, I will have two lumps please, lovely."

I could see Andy and Whiff cringing. Oh no Doggy, I thought, please don't do this, just be yourself mate, you are OK. I'm vouching for you here, you're not only making yourself look like a prat, you're making me look one too, a prat by association.

A few minutes later, with tea served, Ann went back to her kitchen duties, leaving us to sit at the table to slurp our tea and devour the chocolate biscuits.

Dustbin, the Russ' cat, ambled in from the dining room, jumped up onto the kitchen side and began to delicately wash one of his white paws.

Doggy leapt up, put out a hand of peace for Dustbin to sniff, he obliged, then got back to his paw.

"Oh, my word, I love cats, I do," he said to Ann's back at the sink.

"He's a nice natured cat," she said, dipping her hand underneath the wash bowl, searching for any lost cutlery.

"Bloody hell, what a massive cat," said Whiff evenly.

"Yeah, he's bleeding massive in, he?" Doggy said to Whiff, wiping tea off his lips with the back of his hand.

"Oh, he likes you; he might let you stroke his tummy," said Ann, finding two spoons.

"Lovely, that would be lovely," Doggy Godalming–Ed.

I thought fucking hell, surely this cannot get any more embarrassing, can it?

Doggy Kensington Palace-ed, "Oh, I had an amazing dream last night; it was about a cat playing guitar on stage. It was doing a big lead guitar solo… meow, meow, meow, meow," he sang melodically, eyes shut tight, gurning like Dave Gilmore playing 'Shine On, You Crazy Diamond'.

I noticed even Ann, who accepted anyone and anything normally, winced horribly.

"I would love to see a cat onstage doing a big lead," he concluded, to the now totally silent kitchen, even the fridge seemed to have gone quiet.

I thought for fucks sake it's official, I am now a prat by association.

*

I knew it was only three tracks at Thundridge village youth club, but there was a bit of pride at stake here for Dave and me, playing in front of our home audience. Both of us wanted to get it right, make sure there were no silly mistakes, so we decided to go to the hall as early as possible. It would also give Doggy plenty of time to work his magic. Dave collected the key from Bob, picked me up with our gear from my house, and we got to the village hall at about five o'clock, a good two hours before our 'showcase' was due to begin. We checked the gear had survived the trip intact, it had, so we started setting up.

Andy and Whiff strolled into the hall a while later, big grins plastered onto their faces, telling us they were looking forward to the gig, and immediately got stuck in, helping us. Once we had finished, we grabbed some of the Junior Mental Institution or the Junior Mixed Idiots, as Hayley used to call it when she was at the school, chairs off the side of the stage, made ourselves comfortable and waited for Doggy to show up.

"I hope Doggy comes through for us, it could be good," I said, hopefully.

Andy grinned, grabbed my guitar strummed it discordantly and sang, "Tra la la, I'm Dick Van Dyke, I'm gonna make ya sound better than you eva 'ave."

Dave laughed, "Blooming Nora, Miss Poppins and no mistake."

94

"Nah seriously though," I said, "It could be good, he's got some pretty tasty kit at his place."

No one said anything, instead they steadily looked at me, with amused faces.

"OK, OK, I know what you're all thinking, listen he was alright when he was a kid, I knew him at junior school, it's public school that fucked him up."

"Fucking did they," said Whiff, rocking back on his chair.

Dave nodded, "I've never met anyone as messed up as that," almost sounding concerned.

Andy closed his eyes, head up in full lead guitar mode, he strummed, singing. "Meow, meow, meow, meow, meow, meow," at the top of his voice.

"I love seeing a cat on stage doing a big lead," Whiff concluded.

A whole hour went by, and I began to think he had forgotten, or worse still 'mother' had found him something else to do, then finally, thank fuck, the doors burst open and in walks Doggy carrying a black mixer, a selection of small mics and a bulging bag of jack leads. I hoped the others would give him a chance, as not only would it be good for the band's sound if he came through, maybe, just maybe, I wouldn't feel like a prat by association anymore.

Andy, Dave, Whiff and me sat back on our J.M.I. issue chairs watching while Doggy busied himself, powering up his mixer, unravelling leads, positioning the mics around the drum kit.

Doggy then took the leads from the mics, plugged them into his mixer, plugged one into an amp and then with a confident nod of his head, he flicked the switch, producing a low humming sound from my Laney amp.

A high-pitched yowling sound reverberated from behind me, I turned to see Whiff had grabbed my guitar and was a cat on stage doing a big lead. Fuck off I mouthed, shook my head, and turned my attention back to watch our sound engineer, as he placed his headphones onto his head, adjusting the levels on his mixer, hoping to learn something that would help the band in the future.

Doggy knew exactly what he was doing, he moved with stealth, he moved with purpose, he was paced, he was meticulous, he was 'oh shit' taking way, way, way too long, if only he had got here on time, his due diligence would have been fine.

"I'm almost there nah lads, it's a slow process," said Doggy, seeing the frustration on our faces.

A slow process it was. Another half an hour disappeared in the blink of a sound engineer's eye, then finally happy in the knowledge that all of his mics were set up in the correct places for optimal performance, he turned his attention to the amps. Doggy plugged a jack plug into the front of my amp, ran a lead over to Whiff's, where he proceeded to plug it into the front, which didn't look like a good idea at all to me.

"Is that going to be OK? Won't it overload it?"

Doggy swung around testily, pulling off his headphones, "Yes, no, yeah, it's fine, I'm gonna patch the amps in together, so all the instruments will come out of all the amps at the same time… so it'll be like a PA System won't it."

I nodded confidently at the others; our man was on the case; we should trust him.

"OK mate, nice one, looks good."

Once the amps were connected up, Doggy instructed, Whiff, Andy and me to stand by our amps, fingers on the on/off buttons and wait for the appropriate signal to power them up. I smirked at everyone thinking, I'm no prat by association, this is going to be brilliant, watch and learn, ye wankers of little faith.

"OK, on my mark…
Three
two
one…"

Doggy nodded.

SCRRWWRRRREEEEEWWWWWWWEEEEEEEEEEEEEEEEE
EWWWWWWEEEE

A massive scream of feedback erupted, which had us all reaching for our earholes, then the red light on Whiff's amp brightened impossibly, flickered, faded. Died. Whiff gaped, looking down at his extinguished amp, like a mum who had just watched her kid being flattened by an HGV, an HGV that had rolled backwards and flattened it twice.

"What have you done to my fucking amp?" Whiff demanded.

"I haven't done anything to your amp. I set the volume at the right level; you must have touched it," Doggy said, condescendingly.

"Oh, do fuck off, I didn't touch nothing," Whiff told him.

Doggy was about to argue with him, when he seemed to notice that Whiff was not only staring at him with an expression of the purest anger, he was well over six foot tall too, so he dropped his head back to his mixer, nervously twiddling his knobs.

"There better not be anything up with my fucking amp."

Whiff pulled Doggy's jack plug out, chucked it dismissively over his shoulder, leant over his beloved, flicking the switch…

On. Nothing, off.
On. Nothing, off.
On again, Nothing.
Off, on again. On. Nothing, nothing, fucking nothing.

"Why don't you try turning it off at the plug, Whiff," I said hopefully, clutching at straws.

Whiff sighed, pounded past Doggy, dossing out the crown of his head and clicked it off.

A moment passed, he turned it back on again, and praise be, the red light reappeared, shining out on the top of his amp, it flickered once, twice, three times, then returned to normality.

Whiff wasn't done yet, he still eyed Doggy furiously, who had now found something new at the back of the stage to focus on, to avoid his gaze.

"OK Whiff, look we haven't got much time, come on, we need to get ready," I said, trying to calm things down.

"OK," Whiff conceded.

A while later, with our start time rapidly approaching, we heard the thump of the outer double doors opening, followed by the hubbub of people as they came into the hall, so we closed the red velvet curtains at the front of the stage, to give our sound engineer more time to get it right; he only needed a bit more time, he told us.

Doggy stood behind his mixer, sliding slides, twiddling knobs irately in a vain attempt to get it right, it just wasn't happening though. Now, sadly, it was plain for all to see, that whatever he thought he could do wasn't actually possible, the fact was, he was completely out of his depth.

"I'm sorry, I don't know what I was thinking," I admitted to the others.

"Ah, don't worry about it, we'll just play like we do in practice," Dave said, trying to make me feel better.

"No, don't give up yet Skin, I'll go see if I can help him out," suggested Whiff, grinning mischievously.

Whiff plodded over to the drum kit, picked up the floor mic in front of the bass drum, put it to his mouth.

99

"AAAAAAAAAAHHHHHHHHHHHH!" He bellowed.

Doggy jumped backwards, throwing his headphones onto the floor like they were made of white-hot lava, watching them cartwheel off under the drum kit.

"Aaaaaah, ouch, aah Jesus bloody hell," he said rubbing at his ears furiously. "Aaaaahhhhhhh!" he repeated, reaching under the drums to retrieve his cans.

A ruffle of the curtains, Bob's head appeared, "What's going on? Is everything alright? We're ready if you are?" He asked, looking at Doggy's prone form, with an amused look on his face.

"It's fine, Bob," said Dave, uncertainly, still laughing.

"OK, well let us know," said Bob, before disappearing again.

Dave shrugged his shoulders in my direction, I looked in Doggy's direction.

"I'm sorry mate, we've got to go on now, this is ridiculous."

Doggy held up his hand, "No, I'm nearly there."

"No, you're not, it's been a waste of time, mate," I said, fairly.

Impatiently, he disagreed, "No, no, no I'm there now, yes, yes, here we go, I just need to switch this on and…"

SRRREEEEEEEEEDDDDDDEEEEEEEEEEEEEEEEERR
RREEEEEEERRRRRRR

Once again, I put my fingers into my ears, protecting them from the piercing noise, waiting for it to abate and when it did, I heard some laughter behind the curtains.

"Oh, no, no that shouldn't have happened, why did that happen, oh I know what I've done wrong," said Doggy, slapping his head.

"Yeah, and so do I know," I said, then whispering, I added, "having anything to do with you, you fucking twat," under my breath.

Doggy stopped his useless twiddling and looked up at me as if I had run over Faustus, the family cat and chucked his bloody lifeless corpse onto his mixing desk, while grinning like Norman Bates in a taxidermist.

I thought fucking hell he's, his mother.

"You've got to go, this is embarrassing, we are going on now," I insisted.

"Oh, come on now, you didn't really give me a chance," cried Doggy.

"You've had plenty of time, now get off the stage," I said, beginning to lose it.

Bob's head appeared again, "Hello lads, seriously what's going on now? It sounds like the shows already started," he said, laughing at our misfortune.

I smiled patiently, "No, no not yet Bob, sorry mate, can you give us a couple of minutes mate?"

Bob nodded and vanished in a swirl of velvet.

I took a huge intake of air, I thought I'm not losing it here, stay calm. It's fine, everything's going to be OK if I stay calm. I am calm. Each and every day, I'm getting…aahh fuck off… I lost it…

"It's over Doggy, now Fuck off the stage…NOW!!!"

"What about my stuff?" He bleated.

"You can get it later. Now. Fuck. Off."

I wasn't the only one, Andy who had been snarling silently in the wings, watching the farce, getting angrier and angrier by the second, suddenly reached breaking point too, exchanging a grin for his snarl, he set off across the stage pogo-ing, crushing the stupid little floor mics under his size ten, black sixteen-hole Doc Martin's boots. He bounced backwards, forwards, this way, that way, criss-crossing the stage until every last one of the little mics had been vanquished, then turned to Doggy daring him to say something.

Doggy, got the message and got the fuck off the stage, his wisest move of the day.

"OK, come on, forget that knob-end, let's do it!" I said, through tears of laughter.

"Yeah, come on," said Dave, hitting a full kit roll.

Andy casually picked up one of the mangled mics, turned it over in his hand, examining the damage, saw it was good, saw it was totally fucking destroyed, then nonchalantly tossed it over his shoulder onto the small staircase, where Doggy had just made his sharp exit.

Dave shouted that we were ready, the curtains slowly drew back, to reveal the biggest turnout that I had ever seen at the youth club. Seeing us, their mates, up on stage they began, cheering, clapping appreciatively.

"Skinner, Skinner, Skinner!" Little Glyn shouted.

A wolf-whistle followed, there were some laughs, then silence.

Dave hit the two-bar intro to 'Everybody's Boy' and when we all came in, it was lift off, everything was good again, the angst we felt, all the crap we had endured was all forgotten now, as our sound careered out of our perfectly good amps, forcing the silence out of every corner of Thundridge village hall.

'Skinner, Skinner, Skinner' played guitar, Dave lashed into his drums, Whiff's bass rumbled and Andy was at the front, doing brilliantly at cutting out our expletives.

I came to my solo, hit the right notes effortlessly, then smoothly slipped back into rhythm guitar when the chorus came back around; this is brilliant, I thought, we are brilliant, maybe we should do the whole set for them.

One minute, thirty seconds later as 'Everybody's Boy' came to its brutal end, I braced myself for the avalanche of appreciative applause that I knew was coming our way.

Silence, absolute silence, it was deafening, everybody stood statuesque, open-mouthed, gaping at us, unbelieving, wondering, wondering what the bloody hell had just happened.

Colin Hill and Bob Williams, our Youth leaders, began clapping enthusiastically, encouragingly.

A few others eventually joining in.

One and a half minutes, they didn't know what had hit them. I thought no, let's do the showcase set, any longer than that, they'll have to be taken out on stretchers. I smiled to myself at the thought of the paramedics rushing in, tending the dead, the dying and the damned in the little village of Thundridge, crushed under the weight of punk rock.

Dave hit the intro to 'Christ fuckers' or 'C.F.' as Andy had announced it in line with our one-day censorship ruling, as I waited to come in, I began zoning out.

I'd been here before, I was nine years old; I was playing Joseph in the Junior Mental Institution's version of the nativity play on this very stage, all the teachers, all the parents, all of my mates had watched me sing the 'Little Donkey' solo. Now here I was back up here again, only this time I wasn't singing 'Little Donkey on a dusty road' I was singing 'You can fuck your own Christ' - well 'You can XXXX your own Christ'.

Andy's chanting intro ended, I shook off the memory, hit the chords for the first verse. It felt good, I began to relax, as I did so, I took the time to see if this one was going down any better than our first number, surprisingly it was, people were smiling, moving about a bit more. It looked like C.F. with its slower beat was more accessible to

104

the uninitiated. I smiled at the uninitiated; Phil, Taddy, Tom, Lucy, Karen, Seb, Simmy, Mac, Julie, Craig, Danny, Vincent, Glyn, Lee, Mal, Ronnie, Lucy and all the others, as they became accustomed to what they were hearing, nodding their heads in time to Dave's colossal beat.

Cerys was standing at the back and next to her stood Diane, both pumping their arms in the air, I blew them an over enthusiastic kiss, beaming back at me, they waved madly. I wondered how everyone else was doing, Whiff was leaning back hammering his bass, giving his girlfriend Paula Gates a proper show, Dave was completely focused, giving a good account of himself and Andy, what was he doing? I did a double take; it looked like his mic was faulty, broken, cutting in and out, as he left the multitude of Fucks out of C.F. It was comical, an impulse to burst out laughing, rose up inside me, I pushed it down to concentrate on chucking the chords onto the frets again.

Instead of silence, at the end of C.F. people clapped genuinely, a couple of cheers came back too, I thought OK nice one, they're beginning to get us, but we need something, something that unites us all, something to make a real connection.

Andy drew the mic up, "Cheers, this is our last one, it's called 'Protest'… We are dedicating this to Pig Man Cannon… Oink, oink, Cannon fodder."

People cheered, clapped, the connection was made.

Craig and Taddy chanted, "Tit head, tit head, tit head," back to us, people around them fell about laughing, joining in.

"TIT HEAD, TIT HEAD"

"TIT HEAD, TIT HEAD"

Andy began to conduct them like an orchestra.

Bob and Colin couldn't help themselves, they both dissolved into laughter, then realising that some of this might get back to some of the kid's parents, the chant was quickly quelled.

Once the laughing had subsided in the hall, on stage too, I steadied myself, hit the intro chords to 'Protest' and Dave's full kit roll brought everyone in, and it was lift off. Lucy, Julie, Karen, Tom and Phil began pogo-ing at the front, others, soon joined in pushing into them from the back, it was amazing. I hadn't seen such mayhem in the village since Danny and me had kicked in the back doors of the local shop and legged it with all those fags and mags.

A huge cheer rang around the hall at the end of 'Protest', our last track of the showcase, so nodding a thank you to our mates, I went to turn my amp off, only to be stopped in my tracks by Dave hitting the intro to V1 Bomb, I thought yeah why not, they're getting us now. Andy was a fast learner, keen to keep the connection going with our audience when it came to V1 Bomb's chorus instead of bellowing 'V1 Bomb' he sang 'V1, Cannon will be gone', which made everyone in the front row, crack up and bounce with even more enthusiasm.

In the mass of chaotic discord at the end of V1 Bomb, Paula Gates stepped forward and chucked a pair of her knickers at Whiff, who neatly plucked them out of the air and placed them onto his head, which brought the whole hall down.

Bob and Colin pulled the long cords at the sides of the stage, we disappeared behind the red velvet curtains to tumultuous, mirthful applause.

Doggy had disappeared leaving his gear behind, feeling a bit guilty about the whole sad misadventure, I put the stuff that hadn't met a grisly end under Andy's boots into a bag, which I would leave on Doggy's doorstep on my way home. I let out a deep breath, looked around at the other three, it was just like our first gig, everyone was talking, laughing, getting on, it was easy to see why.

Once again, we had acquitted ourselves well in front of an audience, better still, we had gone down well with our mates in Thundridge, so not only was it good for the band's reputation, but it was also good for our personal reputations too. Dave and me were particularly pleased, as it showed some of the more cynical people in the village, the ones who called us yobs, lazy, saying that we would never do anything with our lives, that we could work hard, we could be creative, if it was something that we liked that is, and OK, it might not have been everyone's taste, but that's music for you.

Chapter 7

Work Makes You Free

I had left school and been claiming twenty-five pounds a week from the social security office ever since. It was a lot of money for me, as before the event of the So-Sh I had to rely on the old man, who was always quick to suspend any fiscal payments for anything, nothing and everything, depending on what kind of mood he was in. I received a regular gyro sent through the post every couple of weeks. To begin with, my old man joked that, 'he was getting some of his, Pay. As. You. Earn. Slave. Money back'. It wasn't long before the laughter stopped, though, he told me that he'd had enough of me hanging around the house 'strumming' all day, and if 'I was living in the Soviet Union, I wouldn't get any food, as people who didn't work, didn't eat'.

Whiff and Andy had gone back to school, Dave was working with his old man, and the truth was I was getting bored anyway, so I decided to throw myself onto the mercy of the job centre, see what they came up with. If they could find me something to keep me occupied, not only would it stop the encroaching boredom, but it would stop my old man's constant barracking and maybe, just maybe, I would find something outside of music that I would enjoy doing. I wasn't confident though.

In the end my first job found me, I had absolutely no choice in the matter, as it had come from a busy body friend of my mum's called Mrs. Irene 'Lynched' Lynch. Mrs. Lynched took great delight in meddling in other people's business and was a seasoned professional in the art of being two faced. If she came to visit my mum, she would be all smiles, "Hello Michael, it's lovely to see you, how are you?". If she saw me around the village, however, another face would emerge, she would be all frowns, "Oh hello Michael, still doing nothing are we?" I thought it was hilarious, so I told my mates about it, and sometimes when they saw me hanging around the village they would enquire, 'oh hello Michael, still doing nothing are we?' and we would fall about laughing.

I soon stopped laughing when my mum told me that she had lined up a job for me at High Farm in High Cross. Mrs. Lynched had told her that the wages weren't very good, the hours were long, but she said, "It would be a good start for me, and it would get me out in the fresh air." Oh, nice one, I thought; long hours and shit money, thanks a bunch, you fucking nosey old cow. I couldn't believe her cheek; I wanted to say bollocks to that, but my mum was happy, the old man had stopped moaning, and the farm was owned by Christopher 'Hmm technical, ears pinned back', Patterson's old man who I knew from school. Christopher ars pinned back and me always got on well, we had a good laugh at the Junior Mental Institution, so I was hoping I might be working with him. If his older brother Russell 'The Dennis Healey eyebrows' Patterson was around, though, it could be a problem, as I had humiliated him in the J.M.I. playground. I had randomly picked a fight with him, and he had backed down for reasons unbeknownst to anyone but himself, as he was enormous and would have mashed me to a pulp. I wondered in the intervening years maybe he might have worked that out.

A loud, insistent trilling sound disturbed me from a deep slumber on my first day as a farm hand, my first thought of the day was, to grab the made in Taiwan little plastic bastard of an alarm clock and quite literally make time fly, by lobbing it out of my fucking bedroom window.

Pip, pip, pip, pip. Pip, pip, pip, pip. Pip, pip, pip, pip.

109

It pipped relentlessly at me.

OK, OK, fucking OK, I thought and rolled over, squinting at the red lights slicing through the darkness into my eyes, informing me that it was five thirty am. I didn't even know the day existed at that time, in the what? The morning?

Pip, pip, pip, pip. Pip, pip, pip, pip. Pip, pip, pip, pip.

Still, it insisted.

One swift movement of my hand, I thwacked the made in Taiwan bastard into submission, rolled out of my nice warm, snug, comfortable warm bed and wandered blindly into the bathroom where I splashed some, life reaffirming, ice-cold water on my face, then feeling a little better, I padded off down the stairs for a quick breakfast. Once I had emptied a bowl of cornflakes, had a cup of piss weak tea, I grabbed a piece of stale toast from the night before, spooned a bit of jam on it and left the house, setting off on the two-mile walk from Thundridge to High Cross, chomping awkwardly on it as I walked. I looked on in wonder as the day opened up in front of me.

In the East, a shallow amber sun teased the gun metal clouds, announcing the arrival of a new day. To the West, high up, a toenail moon hung itself out to dry in the early morning sunshine, its shift now over. It was nature in its purest form, as yet untouched by human hands at this unearthly hour. I meandered up High Cross Hill, along the A10 with only the early birds as my soundtrack, arriving at High Farm as the sun burst triumphantly through the gun metal.

I strolled down the track to the farm, enjoying the heat of its rays, and saw Mr. Patterson advancing towards me in his tractor. I wondered if I'd get to have a go in that, that could be a right laugh. Mr. Patterson frowned, pulled up to a halt next to me and flipped the plastic door open.

"Oh morning, I'm Michael Baker."

"Oh right, Mrs. Lynch said you might be showing up," he returned, lowering his portly frame down from the cab.

"Come on then, follow me."

I fell into line behind him, and we marched past a brown stagnant duck pond, through the centre of the farm towards a series of long corrugated-iron buildings.

"It's cold today, isn't it?" I said, pulling my leather jacket into me.

"You'd better start working then, that'll warm you up," he said, dismissively.

"Where's Christopher? Is he about? Will I be working with him?"

Mr. Patterson turned, his face darkening at this idiot that just wouldn't shut up. "No… He's at the university of East Anglia studying farming, and he'll be working now, which is what you should be doing, come on, keep up."

"What about Russell?" I asked, tentatively.

"No, he's not here either, he's a porter at the Ear, Nose and Throat hospital in London."

I stifled a laugh, thinking, well that's the wrong way around, if anyone it should Christopher 'ears pinned back tight' Patterson being a porter at the Ear (pinned back tight), Nose and Throat hospital in London.

"Er, hello, are you listening to me?"

"Yeah," I lied.

"Come on then, keep up."

I nodded quickly and followed Mr. Patterson into one of the corrugated iron buildings, which I now knew to be hen houses. Immediately, I was hit by an obnoxious smell that had me reaching for my eyes, nose and throat as it bleached its way into me.

"Oh, you'll get used to that," Mr. Patterson laughed.

I said, "What?" Unable to hear him over the racket being produced by the caged hens.

Mr. Patterson shook his head abruptly, turning from the idiot who talks but can't hear, and pounded out across the high walkway that cut between the rows and rows of caged birds.

I took in my surroundings, the noise, the smell, the heat that so many birds in such a small area were producing, it was unnatural, claustrophobic, I leant forward, coughing, trying to clear my suddenly parched throat and looked up to see Mr. Patterson's amused face studying me.

"OK, so are ready to stop talking and start working now?"

I nodded, minutely.

Mr. Patterson instructed, "Right then, pick the eggs out of the egg traps under the cages and put them into these holders, not too difficult for you, is it?" Not waiting for a reply, he swept out of the hen house, whistling a little ditty to himself.

Once he had gone, I collected the eggs from the traps, putting them into the basket as he had instructed and as I worked, I glanced into the cages.

In each cage there were five or six hens packed tightly together; close confinement of the poor creatures had clearly taken its toll, some were partially bald as the metal bars had dug into their skinny bodies, others, deformed with legs and or wings, missing. Some looked like they had actually gone insane, standing statuesque, staring into nothing or ripping at themselves constantly, like they were trying to comfort themselves in the hell that surrounded them. On the bottom of the cages, some lay opened beaked, dead, now released from this, the nightmare that their short lives had been.

I hurriedly collected the eggs, loaded them onto the push trolley and took them to the 'egg room', passing the slaughterhouse on the way. Although I didn't want to look, I couldn't help myself, my eyes were drawn to the pitiful rows and rows of pathetic skinny hen carcass' hanging from shiny metal hooks on a long conveyor belt.

Once I had placed the eggs into the large cardboard containers, I stood up straight, stretched the kink out of my back, thinking about what I had just seen, maybe the hanging dead hens were the lucky ones, after all their torment was over.

Mr. Patterson walked in, saw me momentarily idle, "Oh, my word, what are you doing standing around in here?"

"I've just finished, OK?" I said, bristling, lashing out at my surroundings.

Mr. Patterson snorted, "Oh, have you now?" He stated suspiciously.

"Yeah, I have… And do you know that there's a lot of dead chickens in the cages in the hen house," I said, expressing my anger

"Oh, oh, is there now?" He drawled, sarcastically. "I don't think you need to concern yourself with that, do you?"

I thought I'm not going to be able to stand this fucking wanker for much longer, I mean what is his problem, who does he think he is? I know who he is. He's a twat.

"Anyway, so what if they're dead, it'll save me chopping their blooming heads off later, won't it?" He said, belly laughing, conclusively proving my point.

"What do you want me to do now then, I haven't got anything to do."

"What!!?? There's always something to do on a farm boy. Use your initiative, go find something to do, get a broom, clean up," he stormed.

I shook my head at the injustice of it all, trudged off out of the egg room, found a mud encrusted broom, picked it up and began sweeping at some filth in one of the barns.

A couple of minutes later, the barn door crashed open, Mr. Patterson burst in shouting, "What are you doing? Don't do that, do something useful, go and get the feed sacks out of the storage huts near the silo and put them outside the chicken house… And hurry up."

I threw the broom down and pounded out of the barn across a small courtyard, into one of the storage huts, where I began hoisting the heavy feed sacks and lugging them to the hen houses as he had instructed. I had just about finished when Mr. Patterson strode up to me, red-faced, I thought now what? And braced myself for another verbal assault.

"Right, it's lunch. I'll see you in forty-five minutes," he said, cordially, and then he hopped into his tractor and I watched the twat trundle the short distance back to the farmhouse.

I found a bale in the courtyard under the shadows of the silver grain silos, sat down, pulled out my sandwiches and as chewed away, I took in my new surroundings. In front of me, a barn housed what could only be described as a vehicle graveyard, tractors, cars, vans, buses and motorbikes were piled up three high, in amongst them a mass of metal drums leaked out dark fluids into the animal shit and mud beneath. On the courtyard, waves of plastic bags swept backwards, towards them as the wind blew petulantly around the yard, sometimes blowing them onto the vehicles, trapping them, where they seemed to wave frantically as if saying let me go, let me be free. In the background serving as my lunch soundtrack, manic screams pieced the air as the birds still pleaded, pecked and scratched, trying to escape hell on earth.

I was relieved when six o'clock came, at last my first day of work was over. It couldn't have been any worse. I trekked down High Cross Hill, ignoring the beauty of the red sky at night above me, it held no delights for me. Once I was home, I had tea, stayed in with mum and the old man, watching some rubbish on TV, then, at around ten o'clock, hardly able to keep my eyes open, I trudged, upstairs, had a quick shower and went to bed early, to make ready for the next day. It surprised me how long it took me to fall asleep, I was so tired, eventually I succumbed.

I push my hand down on the handle of the metal door; it shudders open, I walk into the cacophony. I stand high on a gantry, stretched out before me; miles of cages, below me, a thousand more. Inside birds screaming, pleading, tearing. Dying. I must release them. My hand reaches out for the latch on the nearest cage, pushes down. It swings open, they rush out, CLAWS raised. Why are they turning? Why are they attacking me, I'm not their capturer? more cages open, birds pour out, vicious, vengeful, the cacophony intensifies, the gantry clicks with the sound of a million clawed feet. I run, I run as fast as I can, I'm not moving, why am I not moving? WHY AM I NOT FUCKING MOVING? The gantry pOUNDs beneath me, they're cOMing, beaRING down on me. I cringe forward, pinching my eyes shut, anTIcipating the pain, then, I'm running in useless air. I'm FaLLing and now, it's ME- SCREaming, it's me PleAding, Torn. Dying...

I woke with a start, drenched in sweat, listening, I heard the cacophony of caged birds calling me, pleading, I shook my head, opened my eyes and all was silent. I shook myself again, still confused in the twilight zone and began unravelling my sweaty body from the sheets. In time, I fell backwards into a fitful sleep, until five thirty am when my alarm clock blew me out of bed again.

116

Pip, pip, pip, pip. Pip, pip, pip, pip. Pip, pip, pip, pip.

"Oh shut up, you plastic bastard," I groaned.

Pip, pip, pip, pip. Pip, pip, pip, pip. Pip, pip, pip, pip. It continued…

An hour later I was back at High Farm again and no surprise, it was exactly the same as the day before, the screaming hens, the mud, the shit, the being treated like shit by Mr. Patterson. I began to think if I stayed here much longer, maybe a week or so, I might even accept him talking to me like that. Nah, I wasn't having any of that, OK, so he was paying me, but there was no need for it, it was like he was trying to break me; that was never going to happen. I won't last much longer here, I thought, I had been pretty shrewd in 'forgetting' to inform the So-sh that I was in full-time employment. I was right, too, the end began when I told Mr. Patterson, about the dead chickens in the cages once again. Only this time to make sure he listened, I said that it might actually be a health risk, people could get ill eating those eggs with all the corpses around, my thinking being if he doesn't care about the animals, maybe he will care about his profits. I was wrong, his response was.

"Chuck them out then, use your brain, you have got one, haven't you?" He abused.

"You can't talk to me like that, who do you think you are?" I responded.

Mr. Patterson stopped in his tracks, surveying me like nobody had ever stood up to him before, "You are working for me, on my farm and I can talk to you anyway I see fit." He stated, raising his voice to stop the rebellion in the ranks.

"Yeah, and you're welcome to it, you can piss off you old bastard," I replied, holding my head up high.

I heard some mumbling about wages as I turned to make my escape, so I shot back, "I'll pick them up tomorrow, and if I was you, I'd leave them with your wife."

I strutted off, hoping that one day, karma would turn full circle and the old bastard would find himself caged, scratching at his own emaciated limbs, looking forward to death.

*

On my return home, I lied low for the rest of the day, but if I thought that would get the old man off my back, I was very much mistaken m'laddo, and with another lecture about the Soviet Union ringing in my cloth like ears I went to the job centre in Ware, securing an interview working as a cobbler for Reg's Shoe Emporium in Hertford.

I met Reg's wife, Wendy, a well-turned-out woman in her mid-forties at their shop and after a short, surprisingly pleasant, interview, smiling broadly, she offered me her perfectly manicured hand, saying I could start as soon as was available.

I was available the next day as it happened, so the next day, I started my second job since leaving Richard Hole grammar school, working for Reg or 'Geppetto' as my co-worker, Mo, called him.

It was the polar opposite to High Farm, I worked in a poky little room at the back of the shop where unsurprisingly, my duties were to repair shoes and then after those shoes had been repaired, I would polish said shoes, sometimes the shoes didn't need to be repaired at all, so I would just polish said shoes instead of repairing and polishing them. An hour of this, I started to believe that I had found the true essence of boredom, there was some rest bite though. Once all the shoes had been repaired and polished or just polished, without being repaired, Geppetto would send me out the front of the shop to serve with his wife Wendy, which admittedly was a lot better than being in the back. I got on well with Wendy, she was OK, a good laugh, could be quite flirtatious sometimes, but if I heard the brass bell ring on the door, alerting us that someone was entering the shop, I would quickly turn away, as if I saw anyone I knew, it would be really embarrassing. Particularly if it was someone from Richard Hole School, as it would be like 'Oh yeah, I knew you'd end working in some shit job like this, Baker'.

A couple of times, Geppetto came into the shop to find his wife Wendy and me sharing a joke, his face would storm over, and I would be banished back into the poky little room to repair and polish shoes, and sometimes just polish them.

Pick up shoe > glue sole or heel > press shoe > polish shoe
Pick up shoe > glue sole or heel > press shoe > polish shoe
Pick up shoe > glue sole or heel > press shoe > polish shoe
Pick up shoe > glue sole or heel > press shoe > polish shoe > repeat.

And sometimes,

Polish shoe

Polish shoe

Polish shoe > repeat.

119

In the end, to amuse myself, I began inventing words to describe the boredom I was feeling by combining, repetitive, boring, tedium, monotony. I soon had loads: repetring, boretitive, monoium, tedotony, but still none of them could quite express the abject tediumonotoboreptativeness that I had to endure working as a cobbler.

It wouldn't have been so bad if Geppetto had something to say for himself, but he didn't, he just got his head down, getting on with the tasks that were placed in front of him.

One day I mentioned it to my co-worker Mo, while we were polishing two pairs of shoes that didn't need repairing. Mo told me to be careful, warning me to watch my step with Geppetto as, even though he was a small bloke, he reckoned he could handle himself, was prone to angry outbursts with very little provocation. I actually laughed; thought he was joking, it was hard to believe, as not only was Reg Wade in the same business as Geppetto with his full head of white hair, white moustache and glasses perched tentatively on the end of his nose, he actually looked just like him. It was hilarious, I just couldn't see Walt Disney's Geppetto throwing punches or sticking the boot in, but Mo assured me he had witnessed it many times over the twelve years that he had worked for him, and if he ever had a go at me, he told to keep quiet, take it, then furtively glancing left and right he leant forward whispered 'Geppetto has problems' into my ear then pulled away nervously, looking around again.

"I'm not taking anything off anybody mate, I put up with it at my last job, and it just got worse," I said, almost truthfully.

Mo shook his head. "Oh dear, that's silliness." Mo leant in on me. "He's... Got... Difficulties," he whispered.

I snorted, I didn't know what he was on about, thought he was winding me up,

"Nah the last time I saw Geppetto he was on TV, he was happy, he had saved Pinocchio from the bad men, it was a happy ending," I said, giving it back.

Mo cracked up, "A happy ending he would like," looking around furtively.

I hadn't heard that euphemism before, so I ploughed on, "I've got a happy ending, for you Moseph old chap, one day Geppetto made his own real boy out of the old shoes people haven't bothered to collect from his shop… The end."

Mo grimaced expansively, putting his finger on his lips, "Shhhh, this is what I'm talking about. He's not just some grumpy old man, he's got problems with you know…" and rolled his eyes.

"What are we going on about, Moseph?" I said, impatiently.

"Oh, for god's sake… I… Er… I… You know… Downstairs."

Oh, shit I see what you mean now, I thought. I was enjoying Mo's awkward euphemisms, though, so I thought I'd keep it going and hopefully in the process I could cover my ignorance. Happy ending!!! How could I have not known that one?

"I didn't know the shop had a basement," I said, seriously.

Mo's eyes flashed red, then he stopped himself, carefully viewing me for a moment. "Oh yes you almost got me there OK, so you see now."

"And Wendy… She hasn't had a happy ending in a long time," I finished for him.

Mo snorted, wagged his finger at me. "I know nothing," he said, in his Manuel from Faulty Towers' voice, creasing up from ear to ear.

"OK… I get it, still doesn't give him the right to have a go at people."

Mo shrugged, "On your own head be it."

A few more tedious days passed, I was still determined not to let my brain die in this sea of monotony, so I started a bit of banter going with Mo in the 'poky' and after a few funny looks, Geppetto told me in no uncertain terms that as Wendy was getting her hair and nails done this afternoon, I would have to man the shop. Cheers you seedless Disney wanker, I thought, a morning of tediumonotoboreptativeness followed by an afternoon of humiliation, and to make it worse I'll be getting paid around two-thirds of what Mo's being paid. I'm a three-times non-winner.

Geppetto, Mo and me sat in an uncompanionable silence, reading our papers, eating our sandwiches through the lunch hour, then reluctantly, at five minutes to one, I waved a sad sarcastic goodbye to Mo, like I was being shipped to Devil's Island with Papillon, and took my place in the shopfront, where I pulled out Sounds and got back to the live review pages.

A few minutes later, the brass bell on the door tinged and Basher shoulder walked into the shop, wearing his infamous hob nail boots. Seeing me, he did a mini double take.

"Skinner!!! What you doing here?" He asked, genuinely taken aback.

"Yeah, I'd like to know the same thing myself, I really would," I parried, realising it was way too late to duck down behind the counter.

"What's up? It's not the hob nails it is?" I asked, doing a decent impression of a shop assistant.

"No, they're fine mate," he replied, moving in on our massive Christmas tree shaped display of Odour Eaters.

"Oi Bash mate, smile you're on camera," I warned.

Basher paused and looked at me with a 'what me' look on his face, "I wasn't going to… it's not connected up anyway," he added, spotting the dangling wires.

"No, it's not," I said, matter-of-factly, "But don't mate, I'm on thin ice as it is."

"Oi, what's going on here then, I can't get anything done back here," an agitated voice called from behind me.

I about turned, there was Geppetto, pipe in hand, glowering at me, over his little frames.

"I'll deal with this," he said, putting his hands on my shoulders, pushing me to one side.

"Yes, what can I do for you, then?" He said, challengingly.

"My sister got some boots repaired here a couple of weeks ago," said Basher, taking up the challenge.

Basher flipped a Reg's shoe emporium bag up onto the counter in one deft movement and pulled out a pair of high black boots.

"See, look at that, the heel's gone again," he said, accusingly.

Geppetto picked one of the boots up. The sole flopped open like a crocodile's mouth.

"Hmm, OK," he said, opening and closing the jaw.

Geppetto pushed his glasses back up his nose, picked the boot up, examining it in the light from the shop's large window, and nodded conclusively.

"OK, we'll redo them free of charge, come back in fifteen minutes," he said, dropping them onto the counter, the mouth shutting with a snap.

"Cheers," said Basher, leaving the shop.

"I wonder what happened there?" I asked, innocently.

Geppetto's eyes cast across me, "I tell you what happened there, shall I? Someone put the wrong bloody solution on there, that's what happened there, see this, see this, see this, see this?" He said, pointing at a crusty yellow compound at the edge of the boots' gaping mouth. "Do you know what that is? That's bloody Therma, that is, it should have been adhesive on these soles, adhesive not

124

bloody Therma," he said angrily, chucking the boots into the Odour Eaters tree, toppling it over onto the window.

"I tell you what, it bloody wasn't Mo or me that did it, so it must have been you, little Mr. Perfect, you're always pissing around showing off in front of people, oh yeah Wendy thinks you're the bee's bloody knees, well I don't, you're sacked!"

I stood gaping like one of Basher's sister's boots, I didn't know what to do or say, then I thought about what Mo had said, and gaped some more. Geppetto moved in close, almost frothing at the mouth, I recoiled from the smell of the cheese and onion sandwich he had eaten for lunch.

"You're sacked, I tell you, … Sacked."

"What? Really? You can't prove that!" I said, cutting in.

Geppetto seemed to be enjoying himself now, he mimicked, "Oh, boo hoo, you can't prove that," In a whiny baby voice. "I don't have to prove anything, I told her we shouldn't have employed you; the place is full of punk rockers now. I bet you're after the glue, not that you could tell the difference between bloody Adhesive and bloody Therma!" He smirked, disappearing into the back.

Geppetto returned with my leather jacket, slung it in my general direction and told me to get out, "I've got some work to do now get out."

I shouted, "You fucking bastard!"

"Oh well done, clever boy, there he is, the real Michael." He laughed, "Now get out of here before I break every bone in your fucking body," he raged, before disappearing into the back.

I heard a rap on the window and Basher's grinning face peered back at me, "You alright Skinner, Geppetto laid into you there, didn't he?"

I nodded, picked up my leather jacket off the floor and opened the door to leave, still clearly shaken up by the twisted Walt Disney characters assault.

Basher put a placating hand on my shoulder, then pushed past me into the shop. "I wouldn't worry about it, Skinner, the cunt's well known for it, he's got cock flop and his missus gets her oats elsewhere, anywhere."

I laughed, "Yeah, I guessed that, it's not my fault though."

"No, it's not mate, come on let's get the cunt back," said Basher picking up one end of the Odour Eater tree, his face splitting into a grin.

"Yeah, fuck him," I said, grabbing the other end, moving towards the still open door.

Once we had navigated our way through the door, we legged up the street, with the display in between us, swinging, left, right, dropping odour eaters in our wake, dodging the many shoppers in Bull Plain, who stopped to see what the two punk rockers were up to. A young couple gawked at us quizzically as we flew by.

"It's my hobnails, I've got really smelly feet," drawled Basher as an explanation, making them break up into fits of laughter.

126

I looked back to the shop, saw a trail of odour eaters leading to it, like we'd dropped them to find our way back to the shop, like Hansel and Gretel.

An anguished cry of "OOooiiiiiiii!!" reverberated all around Bull Plain.

Basher nabbed the last of the swinging odour eaters, putting it into his pocket, we ditched the display and ran off towards Hertford East station.

*

I was enjoying my enforced lie in the next morning when mum called me to the phone telling me it was a woman, my clear head, plus the way my legs were moving, told me it wasn't too early. A glance at my silent alarm clock, told me that it was nine am, I like the way the red glows on its black background this morning. I thought, hmm very nice. I inhaled deeply, pulling the sheets back, jumped out of bed and ambled downstairs, to the phone and grabbed it up.

"Hello Mick, it's Wendy, I was, er… Was wondering if you were OK, it's just that…" she sniffed a couple of times, "Well, are you sick, it's that we're going to need you today."

I looked into the fisheye mirror in the hall, trying to make sense of what I was hearing, only to see my distorted face gawping back at me…. What?

I heard Wendy say, "Is everything OK, Mick?" Gently bringing me back to whatever this reality might be.

"I'm fine Wendy, have you spoken to Reg?'"

"No, not really, no, I need to tell you something...... I..." Wendy sighed, "It's just that Reg... he had a heart attack last night."

"What? No..."

"Yes, there was some trouble in the shop, he... oh I don't know, he must've run out, he collapsed on Bull Plain."

Oh, my fucking god, what have I done, I thought, I should have just walked out, oh no. No.

"Are you there, Mick?"

"No, no, no, I wasn't there, I didn't see anything," I blabbed, totally mishearing her.

"I know, I know, Mick it's OK, it must have happened after you left."

"I'm sorry I didn't hear you right, this line's not too good, is he going to be, OK?" I said, saying a silent prayer for the first time in five years.

"It was about fifty, fifty when they finally got him into hospital, Bull Plain was teeming with people, so it took the ambulance ages to get through, he's picking up now, it'll be a long road, but he's done it before, and he's still... Er... Strong, so hopefully he'll make a full recovery."

I sighed loudly, thank god for that, rubbing my forehead.

"Oh, you really care don't you, aw you're such a nice guy, Mick, you've been so helpful, listen I think I'm going to shut the shop, let things sink in, you'll be on full pay of course and maybe next week we'll reopen, how does that sound?"

"Oh no you can't pay me for not coming in Wendy, I'm thinking of......"

"Oh, Mick, you're like a little light shining in the darkness," she said, cutting across me.

"I'm thinking of…"

"What is it, Mick, you know you can tell me anything."

Oh, fuck this. I thought, this is getting ridiculous, there is no easy way to tell her you're leaving, then again, if I left it a week, as she's suggesting, I could have a bumper pay day of Reg's money, God knows I've suffered for it, and the So-Sh's, as once again I had forgotten to inform them of my new job; tough decision: Greed or Conscience. It was a brutal bout. In the end though, my conscience beat my greed in the tenth round by a knockout.

"I'm sorry Wendy, one of my mates offered me a job working on a farm in High Cross," I lied, putting greed on a stretcher, watching it leave the ring.

"I sort of promised I would do it; you see I like working outside, it's more my sort of thing."

"Oh no Mick, it's been lovely having you around, are you sure?"

"I can't change it now, Wendy."

129

A crossed line twittered something incompressible into my ear, the receiver hummed, I heard a scratching sound.

"OK Mick, well good luck," she simpered, and the line went dead.

I went into the kitchen, slumped down into my chair, scratching my now confused, aching head, hardly noticing that the old man was sitting opposite, hiding behind his newspaper.

"What was that all about?" The old man enquired, dropping the paper forwards like a draw bridge.

"Oh nothing," I said, "It was Whiff."

He snorted, not believing a word of it, "Oh well, unemployed again, what's it going to be today, strumming or sleeping?"

I looked him right in the eye, "Probably a bit of both,"

"Huh," he said, raising the draw bridge.

Chapter 8

Oh Fuck Off Milkman

I had talked to Dave about working for AD on many occasions, as I
liked the idea of working outside, doing different types of work every
day. I had never asked Alan though, as he knew what everyone else
knew, that as soon as Dave and me got together, we would start
pissing about, we just couldn't help it. Dave and me, could be
anywhere, doing anything, we would only have to look at each other,
and that would be it, we would be off. I was still getting flak off the
old man about strumming or sleeping all day at home and Dave had
mentioned how busy the company was, so I cornered Alan while he
was finishing his tea one evening.

"Alan, have you got any work that I could do, I really need a job."

"I don't know, are you sure?" He asked.

I nodded, sure as I could be, and after thinking about it for a while, I
was pleasantly surprised when he said he would be willing to give me
a chance, he needed someone tomorrow as it happened. He also told
me that he couldn't pay me very much, as his margins were tight.
OK, I thought, I won't inform the So-Sh straight away; I'll give it a
few weeks, see how it goes, if it goes well, then maybe, I'll tell them,
if not, no harm done. I hadn't notified them at the commencement
of my first two jobs, High Farm and Reg's, and it had proved to be
the right thing to do as I had been out of them before the ink on my
P46 would have dried.

Dave and me met up at his house early the next morning and took
the short drive to our first job, replacing a slate roof at old man
Dawkin's place at the top of Ermine Street, where we found it was

all prepped, ready to go, as Alan had told us it would be. A ladder ran up the side of the garage, up onto the roof, next to it, sat containers full of felt and battens, all around them, piles of dark grey Welsh slates towered. I walked up to the flimsy looking ladder, shielding my eyes from the early morning sunshine, squinted up to the ridge and as far as I was concerned it was up in the clouds, so I was extremely careful the first few times I wobbled up the ladder into the heavens.

Once I had got over my initial vertigo, I enjoyed the feeling of being so high up and the element of danger that came with it, it was a good laugh scrambling around on the roof. I enjoyed the work too, lifting the heavy grey slates onto my shoulder, feeling the weight on my calves as I took them up the steep ladder over the eves and up onto the roof. My confidence growing every time I deposited a fresh batch of slates, piling them up into stacks onto Dave's brand-new felt and battens, ready for him to nail into place.

In the afternoon, I challenged myself to load more and more onto my shoulders and felt satisfied, as I constantly bettered my last attempt. I loved the burn in my shoulders nearly as much as the feeling of relief when I slid them off into stacks on the roof. I had an amazing feeling of DeJa'Vu and I wondered why, then I remembered humping our amps down to the pavilion all those times and my old man's mirthful reaction as I struggled back up my road.

On the roof, as I piled up the slates, Dave worked hard securing the felt and battens onto the rafters, it was a two-man job really, so once I had shouldered all the slates up, I grabbed a hammer, helping him and while we worked, we took in the fantastic view.

Down Ermine Street, past the Junior Mental Institution, onto the Old Mill House at the bottom, then beyond, up, on the other side of the valley, High Cross, the steeple of High Cross church rising up triumphantly into the clear blue sky. A tree line spread out in a rich green cornucopia of fertile abundance along the top of the ridge, corralling, protecting and preserving Thundridge Village, which nestled at its base.

Sunshine greeted us every morning on old man Dawkin's roof, making the work a lot easier, so much easier in fact, that we finished the job a whole day early, it was a good feeling. Dave and me had talked non-stop, sung the odd twisted version of the kid's Spider-Man song, as we clambered around on the roof, but apart from that we had behaved ourselves, worked well together. I was disappointed when the job came to an end but looked forward to doing it again.

On Friday it was another bright, early morning for me and it being Friday the three of us were in good spirits as we set off for Hertford in the cab of Alan's flat back transit van. Alan, Dave and me travelled along the A10 viaduct over Hertford marshes under a beautiful sunrise; a rich red sun, strobed out golden tentacles into the clear fresh morning air, rising gently, illuminating the earth for the approaching day.

Alan dropped us off at around seven am at our new job, digging a hundred-foot-long trench across a front garden in readiness for a sewage pipe to be laid, which would then connect a new downstairs toilet to the main sewer at the top of the garden. I had never used a shovel before, I learnt quickly though, making sure I used my legs rather than my back to lift the soil and by eleven am we had completed around half of the trench.

Dave called a tea break, so we set our shovels down. I pulled out my bacci pouch and began to carefully load the precious bacci onto a rolly paper.

"Did you hear that Whiff finished with Paula Gates?' I asked.

"What did he do that for? She's alright, she is," Dave replied.

I licked the glue, spun it up and sparked it, spitting out a few errant strands, "I don't know mate, you know what he's like about women, he's obsessed with finding the perfect one."

Dave nodded, "My old man reckons there's no such thing, he says women are like coiled springs, you've got to keep them down, or they'll spring up and BOING they'll get you."

I creased up laughing. "They're like a coiled spring," I repeated.

Dave supped from his teacup. "Oi Skin, you remember Paula Gates' mum at the Junior Mixed Imbeciles," he said pushing his chest out, cupping imaginary boobs.

I cracked up, "Fucking do I, I tell you Dave, I didn't know what they were, or what they were for at the time, but I used to drown in those tits every lunchtime."

"Yeah, me too," said Dave wistfully.

Dave took another slurp of his tea, while I took another look at the ominous looking Hertford police station across the road.

Dave put his empty teacup down, "I meant to tell you, you know you were working at Reg's shoe shop in Hertford, well the bloke had a heart attack, it was in the local papers, I bet that was because you worked for him."

I burst into a nervous hollow laughter. "No, no, no, we were OK, seriously Dave," I protested too much.

"I bet he couldn't take that Skinner stress," he said, creasing up, unaware of the stress building up inside me.

"Nah, we were... er... were OK. What did it say in the paper?"

"Well, he had a heart attack, but he's going to be OK, he'll be out in a few weeks apparently, they interviewed his wife, had a picture of them in hospital, she was well nice, did you meet her?"

Oh, thank you, God or Satan or the Easter bunny or whatever you're calling yourself these days, hallelujah, I thought and yeah, she was well nice, I just couldn't see it under the tediumonotoboreptativeness of the place.

Dave pulled an amused face, wondering where I had got to. "OK, we better do some more Skin," he said, grabbing the wheelbarrow up by its handles, spinning it extravagantly.

"Or no, maybe not" he said, announcing, "Good evening ladies and gentlemen, it's Friday, it's live from the empire ballroom Blackpool, it's the dance of one-hundred-wheelbarrows."

Dave whirled the barrow around himself a couple of times, pulled it in close, dipping it outrageously low. In, out, in, out, shaking it all about, he did the Hokey Cokey turned around, and that's what it was all about, finishing in a flourish with two pirouettes.

I cracked up. "Oh, excuse me, old bean, do you mind if I cut in?" I exclaimed, in a clipped English accent.

"Certainly, old boy," he said, his voice full of gallantry.

Now a Lady, I took the wheelbarrow up and down the garden path, humming the 'Blue Danube' as I held her in my arms spinning, waltzing, dazzling her with my incredible moves.

A while later, we realised that eleven o'clock had quickly become twelve o'clock and even faster twelve o'clock had become one o'clock, so we tossed Lady Barrow aside and jumped back into our shallow trench, having a mad half an hour.

Dave called lunch, we downed tools and wandered over to the local shop where we bought two cans of coke and four boxes of Mr. Kipling's showboat cakes. Returning to the front garden, we settled down at the top, near the road to devour them, whilst taking in the world of Hertford as it went by. Dave was his usual ravenous self, chucking the small yet delicious cakes into his mouth, like Maltesers, barn dooring them one after another.

A little old lady came shuffling along, wheeling her tartan trolley in front of her, stopping at the sight of Dave vanishing cakes.

"Ooh, that'll get inside you boy," she said, quite obviously, and trundled on.

"Naaah, it'll get up my arsehole," replied Dave sarcastically, lobbing a Mr. Kipling's showboat at her retreating frame.

It missed by a mile and hit the back of a car, I creased up laughing, chose my weapon, took aim and bowled another Mr. Kipling's showboat at a passing bus, watching it spin in the air, then flatten itself onto a side window, making a couple of school kids duck in their seats. Dave and me were now in full piss about mode, nothing was going to stop us now. In between taking Lady Barrow for increasingly aggressive spins around the garden, everyone, apart from the police cars leaving the sty across the road who passed us, got caked.

A whole hour passed in a throw of a Mr. Kipling's showboat cake, and a good booting of the wheelbarrow, who we renamed Lady Mud of Mudeford.

In the sky above us, the sun waned treacherously, warning us that the afternoon was almost up, warning us of the impending arrival of Alan who would not only be picking us up, he would be inspecting our day's work. A day's work that had been hampered by cakes and a flirtatious wheelbarrow that would dance with us, but not return to our quarters afterwards for tiffin.

Dave and me grabbed our shovels, frantically digging for all we were worth, arms a blur, sweat dripping, soil flying everywhere. Lady Mud of Mudeford was filled, unfilled, filled, unfilled with impunity as dirt was unceremoniously chucked into her gusset, you never heard her complain though, she showed the true British bulldog spirit. I was totally done in though, my true British bulldog spirit was splattered like the Mr. Kipling's showboat cake on the side of the disabled bloke's three-wheeler car that went by earlier and when Dave told me we were nearly there, we only have another two feet to dig out, I stopped, admitting defeat, I couldn't do any more. Dave wasn't though, his arms were still pumping away in a blur, moving like a man possessed, his face red, sweat streaming from his brow, flying everywhere as his head swung left to right.

"Come on, Skin, we've got to finish it today," said Dave, through great gulps of air.

"OK mate, I'm alright again now," I said, picking up my shovel and ramming it back into the unyielding soil.

A second breath came to me, I became possessed too, displacing the soil in a blur of arms, digging myself deeper and deeper, into the ground like some kind of demented gravedigger. It took us a whole hour to get the trench to anywhere near the depth it should have been, and even then, it still wasn't finished. I was, though, I was done in for good this time, my shovel was now my support, my walking stick. I leant on it, hauling in great deep breaths of air into my lungs, then boggled as I saw the silhouette of Alan's transit van approaching from out of the rapidly setting sun.

"He's back, Dave," I said, through heaving breaths.

"Oh, fucking hell," he said, speeding up even more.

Alan gave us a wave, hopped out of the cabin, came over and looked down at our day's work, nodding his head, satisfied.

Dave stepped back from the trench, "It's been hard work, there was a lot of builders rubble, Dad."

"Yeah, yeah, lots of builders rubble," I whispered.

Alan nodded, a big grin playing at his lips, grabbed a shovel and jumped into the trench, tidied up the edges, then hopped out, to study it from above.

"I think that'll do it lads, well done… Bloody hell, Baker, you looked knackered," he said, grinning at me.

Too out of breath to say more, I managed a mechanical nod.

Alan laughed, "You want to give up those roll ups."

I nodded silenty, pulled my bacci pouch out, "Do you want one?" I whispered breathlessly, offering him a ready-made.

"I couldn't smoke them now," he said, tapping his chest.

"I'm on the Silk Cuts," he said, pulling one out of his pack.

Alan and me lit them up, puffing away, taking in the trench again.

Alan pulled hard on the unresponsive Silk Cut. "It's as straight as a dye, you've got a good eye Skinner."

"Cheers, Alan," I said, flicking ash into it.

Dave walked past us with Lady Mud of Mudeford.

Alan grinned, pointing at her. "And you've got some good dance moves too Skinner, when you're dancing with a wheelbarrow anyway," his face lighting up knowingly.

"Oh shit," said Dave, looking pensive.

Alan laughed, "Bloody old boys, I've been driving past all day."

Dave and me gawked at him.

Alan chuckled. "You should see your faces… You did well at Dawkin's place, finishing a day early, but that's it for the dancing, alright? I'm running a business here, not a bloody finishing school for wheelbarrows," he warned us, and we both nodded, appreciating another chance.

A short drive back to the village, Alan, Dave and me walked back into Ann's welcoming kitchen, a decent week's wage for a decent week's work, followed by a night drinking in The Anchor would be a perfect end to a surprisingly good week, I thought to myself.

Dave and me chatted with Ann in the kitchen, while Alan went up to his office to sort out the wages, returning a few minutes later he handed me my wage packet, I pulled the top off the small brown envelope and saw I had been paid thirty-three pounds for five days' work. Alan watched me carefully and saw my face drop like a tart's knickers, he knew I was expecting more, not a lot more, but more, nonetheless.

"Alright…alright…alright?" He asked.

I nodded, sadly.

"I'm sorry, Skinner, I can't afford to pay you any more, you're not worth it yet. If you learn a bit more, then we'll be able to do something."

"OK, cheers, thanks," I said, too stunned to say anything else and walked out.

Dave followed me out of the house and under the carport. "I'm sorry, mate," he said.

"I'm not working for that kind of money, Dave, no way, man."

"I know, Skin. Look, I'll talk to him, see what I can do. I'll see you down the pub later."

"OK mate," I said, already halfway across the A10.

On the gravel track up towards the churchyard, I did the maths as I walked, and the maths just didn't add up. Social Security were paying me twenty-five pounds a week just to show up at the Job Centre once a week and pretend to look at the jobs on their silly little cards, which was a piece of piss. A couple of hours at most, it took, now I'd just been paid thirty-three pounds for grafting for five days, which meant I had just earned eight pounds for a full week's work. I snorted to myself thinking, there is no way I'm going to give up my free time for that kind of money, eight pounds!! Nah, I want to write music, play music, listen to music and as I vaulted the wall at the edge of the churchyard, I hoped my old man would see it that way too. I wasn't confident though, and prepared myself for another lecture on the gulags of the U.S.S.R.

I thought about it some more after I'd had my tea, settled down a bit, there was no way Alan was going to up my wages just because I was Dave's mate, why would he? Alan was running a small family business, margins were tight as he said, he had already stuck his neck out employing me in the first place, so I wasn't confident that I would be working for AD again. In fact, I knew that would be it, especially after he had caught Dave and me doing what we always did, pissing about. OK, we did the job, but now he knew he couldn't trust us.

Dave and me met in The Anchor later, took our place at the bar, and he told me what I already knew; that Alan was sorry, he wouldn't up my wages until I brought a skill to the company. OK, I thought fair enough, it's only business, I don't care, I'm rich now, it's like I've

141

been paid twice this week. I had my AD money, and my So-Sh money so unfolding a bounty of fifty-eight pounds from my pocket, I told Dave to put his money away; I'll get them in.

Craig and Taddy stalked up behind us, with big grins on their faces.

"You alright Craig, Taddy? You look happy, what's up with you two, is it free pints all night in here for underage drinkers?" I asked, grinning back.

"It's good, but it's not right," said a grinning Taddy.

Craig leant forwards, laughing, "Is that Roy Walker off Catchphrase?"

"Boy stalker off Catchphrase," Taddy corrected.

"Nah, what is it?" I asked, cracking up.

"OK, hold on," said Taddy, taking a deep breath.

"My Mum bumped into Hilary in the shop, and he was going on about all the trouble on the village, and he reckons that it was all down to you, Dave."

"Bollocks," Dave said, bristling.

"No straight-up mate," Taddy countered, smiling broadly from ear to ear.

"Hilary said it's all down to that hypocrite Williams, who needs to sort out who he is before the rapture comes."

"Hypocrite," I said laughing, rolling it around in my mouth, liking the taste.

"The rapture, what is he on?" Dave said, furiously.

"A bottle of vodka from what mum was saying," Taddy replied.

I creased up laughing at the ridiculousness of Hilary; Dave's reaction was pretty funny too.

"It's all down to that hypocrite Williams," I repeated, laughing some more, on the verge of hysteria.

"I wouldn't laugh if I was you Skinner, he said you were a weirdo," stated Taddy, bursting into laughter.

I stopped laughing, "What?"

Dave's face clouded over, "What else did he say, about me?"

"I don't know exactly, mum said he reckoned that you are all sweetness and light when you're working for AD, then after work you change, he said all the trouble in the village is down to that hypocrite Williams."

I said, "Wanker."

"Mum said Dave wouldn't do something like that, and he said, 'oh really well it must be that weirdo Baker then'."

"Fucking wanker," I spat.

I looked at Dave, he was simmering with anger, he slammed his hand down on the bar.

"Nope, I'm not having that, I'm going to go and have it out with him."

Dave didn't bother waiting for a reply, he just got up, marched out of the pub with me close at his heels.

Hilary Charman was the local Parish Vicar, a well-known character in our village, who not only believed in the Holy Spirit, of peace on earth and mercy mild, he also worshipped at the altar of other spirits; namely Gilbey's and Gordon's as his tip of a house would verify.

One day, Hilary could be all sweetness and light, as he walked the path of the righteous on god's green and pleasant land, and you could quite believe he had taken the holy sacrament. Other days though, he would turn into a fully blown, southern states fire and brimstone preacher, and you would actually believe that he had taken a handful of coupons to Oddbins the wine merchants. Hilary would often be seen wandering around the village, white faced, eyes red, blinking unbelievingly, irreverently staring into the abyss, as if a lost sheep searching for its flock. In that condition, people would steer well clear of him, never knowing what he might come out with, particularly parents with younger children as sometimes it was as if Lucifer himself had entered his soul, he would make the little children suffer to come unto him, by scaring them senseless with his apocalyptic tales of Sodom and Gomorrah.

Hilary lived at the bottom of my street, opposite Doggy, with his wife Tamara and the two kids Malcolm and Elizabeth, so I had heard all sorts of stories about the reverend Hilary Charman.

A few years earlier, a rumour circulated around the village that whilst conducting a funeral, he had got the deceased's name wrong, carrying on with the service, despite protests from the mourners, then unbelievably, after the service he had argued with the tear-stained relatives
that it was, in fact them, who had got their father's name wrong.

If that wasn't bad enough, whilst eavesdropping, I heard the old man telling my mum that the Rev held wild parties at the vicarage, as the night went on, the booze flowed, party goers would be invited to put their car keys into a basket and whoever's key they picked out, they could shag them upstairs without consequence. I tried not to think about that one, as the thought of Hilary and his scalp-haired, barge-sized wife, Tamara, drunkenly shagging random strangers at the vicarage would have sent me into everlasting bouts of bilious.

I had my own first-hand experience with the reverend Hilary Charman, too.

A few months after he had moved into the village, when I was around eight years old, I had been seen by Elizabeth Kinnell, Doggy's mum, chucking mud bombs into Hilary's garage, after my old man went around to apologise, Hilary had suggested that I should do the same. In the end my old man agreed with the vengeance seeking clergy man, so did I, when he said that if I apologised to him in person, he wouldn't dock my pocket money for the next two weeks.

I slowly paced the one hundred yards from my house to Hilary's, like a dead kid walking.

Once outside, I weighed up my feeble options.

One. I could lie, tell the old man I had apologised; nope, … A nosy old bag lived opposite.

Two. Lose my pocket money; nope… I was saving up for an Action Man Tank.

Three. Just do it and get it over with. There was no option, it had to be three.

One foot at a time, I drove myself forwards onto the driveway, dodging around two rusty old lawn mowers, a whirligig and a torched Action Man with gripping hands, whose leg was now just a burnt-out blob stuck onto the concrete.

Once I had made it through the obstacle course, up to the door, I pressed the doorbell,

'All things bright and beautiful' chimed out into the evening air.

A moment later, the door jerked inwards, stopped, jammed. A sandalled foot appeared and kicked out the blockage, then fell open to reveal Tamara's huge girth, filling the door frame. Is she wearing my mum's curtains? I thought, as she gazed down at me through thick-lenses.

"Michael, ah yes, we've been expecting you, come in."

"What's this?" Asked Tamara, re-focusing her eyes on a small piece of white paper sticking out of an empty milk bottle on the doorstep, ready for collection by the milkman early the next morning.

A gargantuan paw reached down, plucked the note from the bottle, she read, "Fuck… Off… Milkman."

146

"Oh, fuck off milkman," she said, spinning away from me, excitedly.

"Hilary, Hilary, Hilary, oh fuck off milkman, young Malcolm is getting very expressive with his writing," she shouted back into the house.

No reply was forthcoming, so Tamara carefully placed the message back into its bottle, turning her attention back to the little hooligan on her doorstep.

"What do you want, Michael?"

"Oh, hello…er…my Dad said I should come and say sorry."

"Oh yes, Michael, row your boat in," she said, reversing into the hallway, sniggering at her brilliant wordplay.

I followed her as she deftly weaved her way around pieces of Meccano and Lego, that were strewn all over the floor, then as we passed the kitchen, I peeped inside and wondered why there was a garden chair in the kitchen sink. In the lounge, it became even more hazardous, as in amongst the Lego and Meccano covered carpet, there were marbles, safety pins and needles glinting out from the debris.

On a stripy deck chair in the middle of it all, sat Hilary, a cup of tea, pressed tightly to his lips as he watched a soundless TV. What a strange man, I thought, it's like that program that I like to watch, Stig of the Dump - Hilary of the Dump.

"Sit down, Michael," Tamara intoned and left me to it.

I looked around the room, thought the burst sofa was the best option, and lowered myself down.

"AAAAAhhhhhhh," I said, immediately jumping up again, I saw I had sat on a chicken bone.

"Hilary looked over at the commotion. "Oh yes, give me that," he said, holding out a pale hand.

I handed it over to him, and he absent-mindedly began to stir his tea with it, switching his attention back to the TV.

I fell into line, switching my attention to the screen, weird shapes undulated beneath swaths of thick dust, God only knows what he was watching, so I nervously turned my attention to the room. In one corner of the room sitting high up on an oak dresser a boss-eyed cat, half viewed me, half viewed the TV, and I felt a shiver go down my spine. In the other, a microwave balanced precariously, on top of a trouser press, its door open, revealing a mass of dark red something. I shivered again, hearing movement in the hallway.

"It's Michael," Tamara trumpeted, coming back into the room, with another cup of tea for Hilary, setting it down on an old-fashioned tea chest box, to the side of him.

"You remember he's come to apologise."

Hilary's eyes lifted from the screen, sought me out, and began to bore into me. "Oh yes, the mud bomber, where do you get off?"

I didn't know what to say, I looked down at my plimsolls, hoping this would end soon.

148

"I've got a bucket of worms and a pale of piss for you," Hilary stated.

"Oh, come now Hilary, it was only a bit of fun, he's come to say sorry, haven't you Michael?" Said Tamara the peacemaker.

"A bit of fun, eh? I don't think so, there's a time to weep and a time to laugh, a time to mourn and a time to dance, but there isn't a bloody time to throw bloody mud bombs into my bloody garage is there?" Hilary raged, with furious anger.

Tamara clasped her hands together, "Oh Ecclesiastes 3:1:4, that's very good Hilary, how wonderful."

Hilary smiled contentedly like he'd just proved the existence of God to Richard Dawkins.

"I'm sorry... Please, Mr. Charman, can I go now?" I said, hope, springing eternally.

"Yes, of course you may," Tamara said.

I leapt up and tentatively made my way out of the lounge, dodging the debris as I went.

"You mark my words young man, I will bring down a storm of fire and brimstone onto you if you ever, ever, ever, ever do that again," he warned my retreating body. "Now be off with you."

I stopped my zigzagging and ran like Roger Banister out of the lounge crushing Lego and Meccano under foot, then out into the hall, finally making it to the front door; nearly safe now. I pulled down on the latch, it didn't move, it was stuck tight, I pulled harder, harder, it still didn't give, not an inch.

"Never ever darken my door again," Hilary shouted, as my feeble hands shook, clawing ineffectively at the latch.

It won't open, it won't open, it won't open, I thought, tears welling up in my eyes.

A presence rushed forwards, pushing all the air out of its way, the hairs on the back of my neck stood on end. I gritted my teeth, waiting for impact. Tamara's pink, engorged shovel-like hand brushed across mine, smoothly opening the door. I saw my escape and I ran like hell.

Dave and me reached Hilary's just as dusk settled in, our shadows cast long and wide beneath us as we walked between the two white fences that separates Hilary's house and Doggy's.

"You're the fucking weirdo, Hilary," I bellowed, aiming a kick at the white fence on his side of the path.

A panel split inwards with a huge crack, that echoed between the two houses, "Hilary, wanker, wanker, wanker."

Dave spun around. "No, leave it out, I've got a better idea," he said, determinedly.

Hilary's light-brown Citroën, sat on the drive, doors and boot gaping open, like the passengers had to make a quick exit.

"Yeah, watch this…"

Dave casually strolled over to the car, hopped into the driver's seat and fastened the seat belt, "Oi Skin, come on push me, let's go, come on."

"Oh what, really?" I said, cracking up.

"Shh… Quiet, push me, push me, come on."

I creased up laughing, ran over, put my hands on the boot, smudged a deeply encrusted layer of dirt and saw the Citroën was actually dark blue.

A loud creak told me that Dave had let the handbrake off, so I put my weight onto the car. It eased forward down the slope of the drive, out onto the street where we started picking up speed. By the time, we passed the huge oak outside the Harrington's house, Dave told me the speedo was almost touching twenty miles an hour.

"OI, OI, BLOOOODY HEEELLLL STOP, STOP, STOP!" Hilary cried behind us.

Dave threw open the driver's door, jumped out, abandoning the car, it freewheeled up the street for a while, then bounced into the curb, screeching as the wheel trims scraped hideously along the concrete stone before it finally came to rest.

A dark presence, pelted out of the twilight, towards us, metal blakeys on its shoes click-clacking menacingly on the tarmac, throwing up sparks.

"I'll do for you, you ruddy swines!"

Dave and me legged it passed the jettisoned car, onto the relief road

151

at the side of my house, into the pit round the back, where we laid low, waited, laughing, listening.

Hilary's car door slammed, the engine exploded into life, it screeched off up the road, past Ian Simm's house, slowly fading into the distance.

A moment later, the soft hum of an approaching car became a roar as Hilary's motor skidded around the corner at the top of my road, thundered down the straight, then with a screech of rubber on tarmac, it came to a halt outside my house. I heard voices.

"What the fuck is that silly bastard doing now?" I asked Dave.

"I don't know, but it's too good to miss, let's go and have a look," he said, laughing.

I nodded, smiling at the audacity of the bloke, with Dave following close behind me, I vaulted the fence into my back garden, ran around the side, out into the front, ducking down behind the rose bushes underneath our lounge window, listening in.

"I don't know what you're talking about." It was Phil.

"I want to know who stole my car, was it you?"

"I told you no, Mr. Charman," said Phil, patiently.

"Whoooo stole my car? Who stole it? Who stole it? Who bloody well stole it, then?" He said, stamping his blakey's onto the tarmac, producing more sparks.

"Oh, for God's sake nobody's stolen it, it's there in front of you," said Phil, pointing at the car on the Harrington's front lawn.

"Oh yes, very clever, 'for God's sake' you say, let me tell you this, he's forsaken you, oh son of Sodom."

"I don't know what you're saying," Phil cried.

"I'll tell what I'm saying, shall I? I've got the fires of Hades burning for the thieves who stole my bloody car, hells bells are pealing out their names."

Cockadoodle dooo!

A cockerel crowed its evensong in the distance, Hilary froze, then whispered, "Aah yes, the cock has crowed, are you a Peter or a Judas in my midst?"

"I'm sorry Mr. Charman, I have to go, I'm meeting a friend," said Phil, backing off, clearly unnerved now.

"A friend, a Roman, all will be even at the end."

"You're a bloody fruit cake, you are. I'm going."

Phil turned, fast walking away from this bloody loony.

"Oh yes, run away, even the youths shall faint and be weary and the young men shall utterly fall," Hilary preached at the lost sheep.

"Sod off, you nutter," instructed Phil.

Hilary jumped into his car, wheels spinning, he backed it off the

Harrington's grass, cutting it up even more, and cruised alongside him, barracking him.

A window sprang open above us, a torchlight blazed into our eyes.

"What the bloody hell are you two doing down there?" My old man demanded.

I looked at Dave's grinning face. I couldn't resist it.

"I'm just getting the green fly off mum's rose's, Dad!"

"Piss off," said the old man, stifling a laugh, and the window closed with a thump.

I looked down the road, saw Hilary's car reversing back onto his drive, the door opening and immediately slammed shut again.

Dave said, "I think he's had enough, don't you, let's leave it now."

"I reckon that's a good idea mate, come on let's go and have that pint now, maybe see Phil," I laughed.

Dave nodded and went to walk back down my street towards Hilary's.

"Oh what, no come on, Dave, let's go the long way around."

"Huh, I'm not wasting my shoe leather on that twat, come on," he said, adamantly.

"Really?"

"Yeah, come on."

I snorted, "OK, it's up to you, mate."

Dave and me tentatively made our way back up my road, passing the carnage of the Harrington's grass, passing the huge oak, passing Doggy's pampas grass.

"I don't like this Dave, have you ever heard that expression about criminals always return to the scene of a crime?"

"Yeah, what about it?" He said, scratching his chin.

A car engine turned over, a blinding light bisected us, full beams blazing, Hilary's car shot off his drive, wheels screaming, coming at us like a bat out of hell, bearing down on us.

Dave yelled, "Oh fucking hell, Skin, run!"

Too late I already was, I sprinted past the pampas grass, past the Harrington's, past the oak tree, past the spot where we jettisoned the car and past mine, finally stopping at the relief road, my heart pounding in my chest and I looked back. I thought this is getting out of hand now, I don't care what Dave says, I'm taking the long way to the pub; Hilary's unhinged.

A moment later, Dave came skidding into the relief road next to me, bent down, collected a handful of gravel and as Hilary came racing by, he let loose a barrage of shingle peppering the side of the car, some entering the driver's window. I heard a muffled cough, a roar of pure anguish, the wheels screamed as Hilary slammed the anchors on and the car fishtailed, skidding down the road, finally coming to a halt at the top of my road, we stood panting waiting for his next

155

move. Hilary didn't know what his next move was, he just sat, engine idling, now and again putting his head out of his window, to spit out gravel.

A couple of minutes later, Hilary made his mind up, the reverse light popped on, the Citroën performed an awkward six-point turn and then slowly coasted back towards his house, a defeated man, we breathed easy, the rapture was over; for now.

*

Dave and me were back at The Anchor the next evening, making up for lost time, when Phil came in, joined us, and we told him the story.

Phil smiled, nodding his head thoughtfully. It all made sense now.

"I heard you two had gone up there, so silly me, I went looking for you, I was walking up your road Skinner minding my own business when Hilary came racing around the corner, saw me, swerved off the road, up onto the pavement and came skidding across Harrington's grass, he almost hit me, the nutter was inches away."

Dave and me creased up laughing at the image of Hilary's Citroën mounting the curb coming at Phil, like a character from the Mad Max film.

"Oh, you bastards, I thought that fruit loop was going to kill me, he was frothing at the mouth, and now I know why… you bastards."

"You fancy a pint, mate?" Dave asked the god bothered Phil.

"Cheers, Dave," he said, smiling.

"We'll get them in for you tonight, Phil."

Well, it was the least we could do.

Chapter 9

Mucky Pup

I felt it was time to give the aggro in the village a rest, after our run-ins with our psychopathic vicar and the overzealous policeman; both of them were delusional, and one of them had shown themselves to be dangerous, homicidal, even, so it was time to find something else to get into. Dave and me always liked a drink, so we spent most of our time in either The Anchor, drinking with Craig and Taddy or in The Brewery Tap in Ware drinking with Whiff, Andy and the assaulted reprobates and rockers who frequented 'The Tap'. I loved the pub atmosphere, meeting new people, finding out what music they were into and best of all having a few snakebites with them; alcohol always broke down the barriers, opened people up, usually by closing time you'd be talking to strangers like you'd known them all of your life.

It was expensive drinking every night, but I had a decent amount of money in my pocket after my little flurry of jobs and because of my failure to secure full-time employment to placate the old man, I was doing a bit of gardening for Mrs. Grubber, an old German widow, who lived in a huge house outside the village. Mrs. Grubber not only paid well over the odds, she paid cash in hand too, which meant that the lovely people at the So-Sh were totally oblivious, so I still received their contributions, thank you very much.

Cerys and me hadn't seen each other for a while as we had fallen out over the amount of trouble Dave and me had been causing in the village, particularly dumping the road signs into the river. She had been seen out and about in Ware with Maxine Weir, a friend of hers from her old school, and a couple of other punks. Dave never had any problems with girls, so once we started hanging out in The

Anchor regularly, it wasn't long before he started going out with a nice-looking blonde girl, Stephany Saunders. Steph's younger sister Jill was good looking too, I had seen her around the village walking the family dog, and we had said hello a couple of times, so I asked Dave if he could get her to come to the pub with Steph and Dave, being the mate he was, said he would see what he could do.

Both girls seemed prim and proper, particularly Jill, who looked like your quintessential yuppy with her Diana wedge cut and lose canvas slacks, so I didn't expect her to come, I doubted whether she would want to be associated with a punk rocker with my reputation. Dave came through for me, though, and she showed up with Steph on their next date in The Anchor.

Once we had got the drinks in, Steph led Dave away to a different snug, leaving me and Jill on our own, which I found a bit daunting since I hadn't really spoken to her before. I need not have worried, it didn't take us long to find some common ground, we were soon enjoying each other's company, and although she wasn't as confident as her older sister with her 'why does it always happen to me' attitude to life, she had a great sense of humour and a body to match.

Over the next couple of weeks, on most evenings, we walked out into the countryside with her brown and white British Bulldog, Benson, getting to know each other, it didn't take long. I couldn't believe how quickly it happened; we were so different, the punk rocker and the Yuppy girl. Jill was the same, it was a total surprise, we felt like two totally different worlds had come together, in a beautiful way, and we were soon holding hands or linking arms.

I realised two things.

One. I liked Jill; she was an amazing girl. I wanted to go out with her, so much so, that I started thinking about how and when I was going to ask her.

Two. I hated Benson, her dog; he was a total asshole, so much so, that I started referring to him as Bentsod when I was talking about him with my mates.

Bentsod was untrained and spoilt rotten, after every meal he was given a bowl of milk, a whole pint, so when Jill put his choker chain on and took him out, inevitably he would puke it all up again.

One minute Jill and me would be strolling along arm in arm, chatting, laughing, joking around, enjoying the moment, getting closer, then the next, Bentsod would go into convulsions, choke, gag and regurgitate a warm milky flux of spew all over the place. Immediately, a clearly distraught Jill would drop to her knees, patting, stroking, comforting, healing her little angel, all the while cooing 'Aww… What happened to my little boy?', 'Aww… You poor baby, what's happened?', 'Aww… Are you feeling poorly?', 'Aww… My prince', 'Aww… Little Ben, Ben'. Aww… Aww… Fucking Awwwwww.

In those moments, I stood well back looking on, lip curled up, stomach doing somersaults, thinking, Jeeesuurrs I'm going to be sick myself in a minute.

Jill would then take a handkerchief from her jacket pocket and mop up the drool from his jowls, neck, paws, anywhere the spraying flux had fallen, before he could start eating it all over again. Bentsod was so keen to gurgitate his regurgitations, sometimes she would get shirty with him and pull him by the choke chain, which inevitably lead to another blast of frothy gut milk.

Once Bentsod was all ship shape and shiny again, Jill would shove her handkerchief back in her pocket again ready for the next eruption and roll her eyes at me expansively, as if a put-upon mum, and we would get back to our walk again. I felt weird having watched that, even after the queasiness had gone, something wasn't right, was it a window to the future? I didn't know. One thing I did know was that I couldn't stop her taking her dog out for a walk, just because it made me feel like vomiting, myself, she loved the bloody milk expelling pooch, they came as a package, so when it all came down to it, I had to ask myself one simple question.

To be with Jill and Bentsod, or not to be with Jill at all. Jill was funny, had an incredible body, and the fact was I still wanted to go out with her.

A couple of times the moment seemed right to ask Jill out and on both occasions with my mind screaming, go, go, go, I had fumbled, stalled, bottled out and the moment had gone.

One morning, I steeled myself, thinking that whatever happens, I'm going to ask her out today, no matter what. It turned out to be the perfect day for it, it was beautiful, the sun shone down, radiating its warmth into the rib valley. A rich smell of flowers rode on a gentle late summer breeze, coming from the south of the valley. It couldn't have been any better.

I took Jill down to the river, we walked arm in arm along the track at the water's edge, watching swarms of mayflies dancing on its shimmering surface, then I turned to her.

"I really like being with you, Jill," I said, holding her hazel brown eyes.

"I know you do; I like being with you too, Skinner," she told me, smiling.

"Who would have thought it, the punk and the yuppy eh?"

Jill beamed at me, leaning in, squeezing my arm affectionately.

I thought, this is it. Go, go, go.

HUK, HUK, HUK, HUK, HUK, HUK!

Bentsod choked, retched and blasted a geyser of warm milky drool into the shimmering water, white-washing two mating damsel flies. Jill's hazel brown eyes disappeared, she went down, fussing over him.

"Aw what happened to my little Ben, Ben, hmm? You poor little soldier," she said, dabbing at him with her crusty hanky.

I looked at the bloody thing with its milky bib dripping onto the riverbank and I swear it was grinning up at me. You little bastard I thought, you did that on purpose, it's personal now. I'm going to go out with her no matter what, so I steeled myself, to go again, waiting for the drool to be cleared, then I heard a shout, looked up and there was Dave and Steph waving, walking up towards us. I waved back, pulling an inane grin on my face, my moment really had gone now.

In the pub later that night, I told Dave of my suspicions.

Dave snorted, "What? You think you're in competition with a dog?"

"Yes, I fucking do mate, I wait for the perfect moment, and then he explodes like Marc Almond after a big night out," I ranted.

Dave choked on his pint, as it went down the wrong way, almost spitting it back out again.

"Oh, fucking hell, Dave, don't you start with it as well," I pleaded. "Bloody hell, have a heart, mate," I Alan-ed.

"In competition with Bentsod, maybe you should lay off the snakebites tonight Skin."

"Hmm, yeah maybe, anyway, it looks like it's going better with you though?"

Dave nodded, telling me that Steph was an amazing girl, a good laugh, intelligent, then leaning into me, he told me she was a real goer in the sack.

"Yeah? Cool, she puts the fanny in Stephany, does she?" I joked.

Dave smiled, took a swig of his pint and told me they had already tried a Russian kiss.

"Yeah, what's that, then?" I asked.

Dave explained, "The girl gives you a blow job, and you cum in her mouth."

OK, that sounds good, I thought.

He continued, "Then you kiss, and she gobs it back into your mouth."

Nah, no returns, I thought. If I've given a porridge of little Skinners away to some lucky girl, I don't want them back, no chance, they're hers to keep.

"You should persevere with Jill, you know," Dave advised.

I nodded, "You reckon she's a goer as well then?"

"I don't reckon, I know Skin," he informed me, grinning like the Cheshire Cat.

I chuckled, "Bollocks."

"No seriously, I got off with her at a party at Chadwell Springs Golf Club, I thought I told you?"

"No mate, you didn't," I said, feeling deflated.

"Yeah, yeah, we fucked in the sand trap on the 9th hole."

I cracked up, "I hope you raked it over afterwards, that would be a hell of a lie, wouldn't it? In Jill's peachy arse groove."

On the way home later that night after closing time, I thought about Dave's disclosure. I remembered that every time I had mentioned Dave to Jill on one of our walks, her face seemed to change, she'd become wistful, dreamy even, talk about him in an almost loving way. At the time I didn't give it much thought, as a lot of girls seemed to talk about Dave in that kind of way, but after Dave's revelation, it all began to make sense.

Jill not only wanted to go back to the links with him for another round, but she wanted to be with him all the time, she loved him and now, her big sister was with him, it was a great big mess. I felt sorry for her, began to understand her 'why does it always happen to me' attitude, for Jill and me it was impossible now, so I stopped going out for walks with her, and although I missed her pretty smile and her warped sense of humour, I didn't miss the little milk Vesuvius Bentsod.

I consoled myself by thinking about our next gig; Andy had told us at our last practice that he found someone who could get us regular gigs, the first one being in a couple of weeks' time, at a place called Founder's Hall in Ware, where he had played with his previous band Necro, he reckoned as it had been a CND benefit, they had a decent sized crowd in. It was great news, just what I needed, I loved the build up to the next gig, the excitement, the apprehension and best of all, the last practice before the gig. Andy, Whiff, Dave and me would always put so much more effort into it, knowing a gig was imminent and that in turn, would lead to a real feeling of unity within the band; it was our rallying call.

A call Dave seemed to miss, this time, as a few days before the practice he told us that he was stopping over at Steph's house the night before, which none of us were happy about. Dave had done it before, hadn't showed up the next morning, so I had to go around Steph's to door knock him out of bed, which took ages, my incessant banging usually waking up the neighbours long before disturbing him from his slumber.

Once I had managed to get him up, get him moving, get him to the pavilion in front of his drum kit. He was so knackered, we didn't know whether to put his drum sticks in his hands or under his eyelids to keep him awake, and after what he had told me in the pub,

I knew why. Dave didn't get any sleep, sleeping around at Steph's. I thought jokingly that he probably worked harder sleeping over at Steph's at night than he did with AD during the day.

On the Friday night at our unofficial practice at pavilion, I swore to myself that I wasn't going to let it happen again, I wanted a decent practice before Founder's Hall.

"Dave you will be here tomorrow morning won't you mate?" I said, almost pleading.

Dave laughed, "Yeah of course I will, don't worry, I'll set the alarm clock myself."

"You sure, I mean we can start later, if you want?"

"Skin. I. Will. Be. Here."

"I don't know, maybe I should have the key?"

"I'll be there, Skin, don't worry about it, you worry too much."

"Well, some bugger has too," I my old man-ed back.

Dave shook his head. "Seriously, I will be here," he insisted.

"Nice one man, it's going to be a good one."

"I'm really looking forward to it, a last practice before a gig, everyone will really be going for it," Dave said, sincerely.

*

On Saturday morning, I walked down to the pavilion to find it empty, locked up; there was no sign of Dave.

I sighed, shook my head, walked around the back of the pavilion and across the field to the river rib, pigeon stepped, balancing, crucifix like across the large drainage pipe that spans the river and up into Dellfields where Steph lived.

BANG, BANG.
I hammered the door knocker impatiently, waited, no answer.
BANG, BANG, BANG, BANG.
I hammered the door knocker testily, spat on the grass, no answer.
BANG, BANG, BANG, BANG, BANG, BANG, BANG, BANG.
I hammered the door knocker angrily, head spinning up to the bedroom window, still no sodding answer.
BANG, BANG, BANG, BANG, BANG, BANG, BANG, BANG.
I hammered it again, net curtains ruffled in a downstairs window next door.

One more and I'm going, I thought. I grabbed the knocker aggressively, pulled it right up and the door fell inwards, taking me with it, almost pulling me into the porch.

I stepped back. Bentsod's grinning face greeted me from behind the thermal door curtain, in the hall, his tail wagging happily behind him. OK you won, I thought, laugh it up you little bastard; I don't want her now anyway, not after she changed herself into a par one for Dave at Chadwell springs golf course.

"Oh, Skinner," Steph spat, huffily pulling her dressing gown around her.

I wanted to say 'is Dave coming out please' I thought better of it.

"Do know what time it is?" She asked, impatiently.

I thought, yeah, I do it's practice time, but a bit of diplomacy was needed here.

"Hi Steph, is Dave up? We're practising today," I said, knowing that hassling her would just slow things down even more.

Steph snorted, looked up to the heavens, rolled her eyes. "OK, OK, OK, I'll tell him, I'll tell him." she scalded, before slamming the door in my face.

A curtain in the neighbour's house ruffled again, only this time, it pulled all the way back to reveal a middle-aged woman wearing a green hair net, scowling at the weirdo punk rocker, standing, well, anywhere near her, or her lovely house. I put up my hand, giving the alien a sarcastic little wave, before marching back towards the pavilion, presumably her eyes like daggers stabbing my back as I went.

Steph, why was she so off with me, I thought, what have I done wrong? I could understand people being off in the morning, I wasn't a morning person myself, but it was all the time; this feeling of, keep away, Dave doesn't need friends anymore, he's with me now. I remembered a conversation I'd had with Cerys when Dave had first shown an interest in Steph. Cerys told me that Taddy her older brother had gone out with Steph and in a drunken moment, he had not only told her about Steph's huge sexual appetite, which he said was draining, he had also mentioned how possessive she was. Taddy reckoned that it didn't matter what he was doing, whether it be fishing, football, the pub, even accompanying him to a job interview, where she waited outside like another, interviewee; Cerys said he felt

168

like he couldn't go anywhere, do anything, see anyone without her being at his side, and it was pissing him off.

I concluded, "So all that action comes at a price then?"

Cerys had laughed, "Yeah, it looks like it."

Oh well, I thought, it's not the worst exchange in the world and Dave's not Taddy, Dave knew how to look after himself where girls were concerned.

Whiff and Andy weren't due for another hour, so after crossing back over the pipe, I wandered to the local shop to get some rizlas, in the process of burning up some time. A nutritional breakfast of two Mars bars, a can of coke, followed by a roll up using my fresh packet of rizlas and the world looked a better place.

I strolled over to the bridge, leant over the edge to view the underwater traffic lights, or the Thundridge illuminations as they had been christened. In the daylight they didn't look so impressive, their insistent flashes shimmering on the top of the dark green water, blending in with the early morning sunshine. In amongst the strobing lights, I saw with some sadness that most of them had succumbed to the deep water, were just shadows, underwater shadows, of their former selves.

"You alright Skinner, what are you doing up so early, did you shit the bed?" Asked Phil, walking up behind me, disturbing me from my contemplations.

"Oh, alright Phil, yeah, yeah I did, your mum didn't mind though, she reckons she'll just sleep on the other side tonight." I parried. "What about you?"

"I'm working with AD today," he said.

"Whoa, what are you going to spend all those wages on, Phil?" I said, coming out with the standard village joke.

Phil cupped his chin thinking of all the possibilities, "Hmm... I don't know, maybe a yacht, a Ferrari..."

"What made by Airfix?" I scoffed.

Phil laughed, "You know, Skinner, the money I'm earning today, it'll only be the glue."

I cackled back at him.

"No, no, it's getting better...getting better," he claimed, feeling a bit guilty.

"I hope so, mate," I said, drawing a line under it.

Phil Hilary-ed, "So where is that bloody hypocrite Williams today? He's not at the house."

"Oh, he's still at Steph's, he spent the night over at hers."

"I've got a bucket of worms and a pale of piss if I see him around my house... mark my words... that bloody hypocrite Williams," Phil Hilary-ed some more.

"The cockerel has crowed, are you a Judas in my midst?" I Hilary-ed back.

"A friend or a Roman?" Phil Hilary-ed forward.

"Hells bells are pealing out their names" I Hilary-ed back, cracking up laughing.

Phil and me ping-ponged Hilary around for a while, then finally putting the irreverent reverend to sleep, Phil said, "Dave's been staying over at Steph's then, oh well, at least it's going OK for one of you."

"What do you mean?" I exclaimed.

"Shit, you don't know, do you?" He said, slapping his forehead.

"Know what Phil?" I insisted.

"Dear oh dear I… Well I heard that Cerys is going out with some bloke in Ware."

I felt a stab of jealously, "Who told you that?"

"Hayley did, a couple of days ago," He explained.

I scratched at my forehead, trying to remove the thought. "Nah she wouldn't do that," I blustered, with no confidence whatsoever.

Phil pulled a grimace onto to his face, awkwardly gazing off into space, hoping the messenger wasn't going to be shot, while I tried to digest what I had just been told.

"I need to talk to Hayley now. You going back up to Dave's?" I didn't ask, telling him he was.

"Of course, mate, I'll drop you off," Phil said nodding, relieved that they'll be two messengers now, maybe I'd shoot the other one.

A sleepy Hayley told me that Cerys had got so pissed off with being 'messed about' by me, when a punk friend of Maxine's, Mark Palmer, had asked her out, she had said yes. I felt a stab of jealousy rip through my veins all over again, and I thought if I see this Mark Palmer wanker around the village, I'm going to kick his fucking head in.

Whiff and Andy showed up at Dave's a while later with a half-asleep Dave in tow, and after a quick cup of tea in Ann's kitchen, we walked down to the pavilion together for our last practice before the gig. It was a beautiful day, the others were enthusiastic, talking, taking the piss, laughing and even the knackered-out Dave was getting into it between yawns.

I was confused. Angry. Jealous. Anxious. Frustrated. All at the same time, the beauty of the day and the carefree laughter of my mates, made it worse, just adding to my anguish. It all seemed to be mocking me somehow. I thought what a bastard that Mark Palmer character is, steaming I like that, but then the rage subsided when I thought. Why hadn't I just asked her out? I'd had plenty of opportunities, but just like Jill before, I hadn't done it. Why, why, why, but why? I couldn't even blame it on that milky mugged mutt Bentsod this time. I said to Whiff, I was having too much of a laugh with my mates, I didn't want to commit to anyone, I won't ask her out just yet, there's plenty of time- I actually said that!

Once we got playing, I was still thinking about the injustice of it all, 'I didn't want to commit to anyone' kept spinning around in my mind, taunting me. I didn't want to bring anyone else down though,

172

they were enjoying themselves, reveling in the last practice before our next gig, so I put a brave face on it, grit my teeth and smashed the chords even harder onto my fret board.

A few over keen, Thundridge United football players arrived early for their home match that afternoon, so we packed up a bit earlier than usual, despite my feelings it had still been a decent practice, and we were more than ready for the Founder's Hall gig next Saturday night.

Whiff and me went back to mine for our regular smoke and jam session, leaving Andy to walk back to Ware to go to his boxing club, and Dave to sleep off his night shift.

I told Whiff what had happened with Cerys.

"I wondered what was up with you, I thought you were going to start playing ballads at practice," he said, laughing.

"Fuck off Whiff, I'm in pieces here, man."

"Yeah, sorry man," he said, putting his hand up as an apology.

"You know all the punks in Ware, who is this Mark Palmer wanker?"

"I was wondering when that was coming, yeah, I know him."

"Tell him from me, he's going to get a fucking good kicking," I said, spitting fire.

"Nah, sorry Skin, I'm keeping out of it."

Whiff took a puff of his rolly and blew out a funnel of smoke, "I know you don't want to hear this right now, but well... well I've known him for a long time, and he's alright... and well... you'd like him as well."

"Huh... I doubt it."

Whiff moved uncomfortably in his seat, "It's not really his fault though, is it... I mean, you weren't going out with her... And... Well, you were thinking about asking Jill out."

I nodded, "Yeah, I know, I know, I had plenty of chances, it's doing my fucking head in."

"I know mate, look I know him Skin, and if he had known you had something, going with Cerys he wouldn't have asked her out, he's not that type of bloke, if you meet him, have a chat, you'll see he's alright."

*

A few days later I saw Mark Palmer with Cerys and his little brother Gobber in the square, sitting in front of a boom box, blasting out The Clash's first album, heads nodding in unison. Cerys looked up apprehensively as I shouldered up to them, Mark's face was unreadable though, which meant one of two things to me. One, he didn't know that I thought Cerys and me had something going on, or two, he knew, and he didn't care.

"You alright Cerys?" I spat, accusingly through tight lips.

"Yes, I am, thank you very much," she retorted.

"Who's this then?" I said, eyeing Mark.

Mark Palmer stood up; hand outstretched, smile stretched even further.

"I'm Mark, Whiff knows me, he's told me a lot about you Skinner, he reckons you like The Pack?" He said, pulling out a cassette tape and handing it over.

"What's this then? "I said, turning it over in my hand, "Oh what, I've been trying to get hold of this for years." Seeing it was The Pack's rare live recording, commonly known as Donut 1 cassette. "Fucking hell, it's got 'Legion' on it!" I said, excitedly.

Mark laughed, "Yes mate, side one first track, it pisses over Theatre of Hates' version, you want to listen to it?"

"Yeah," I said, proffering it to him.

Mark took the cassette, slipped it into the boom box, banged up the volume, pressed play and the first orchestral type cuts of The Pack's version of 'Legion' echoed around the square.

I thought, fucking hell, that's brilliant. Fucking hell Whiff was right, he is a decent bloke.

Cerys sat back, an amused look plastered onto her face as she watched Mark, Gobber and me unite over our love of punk rock music.

The Pack's 'Legion' finished to rapturous applause from the audience in Brixton, and even though it was a rough recording, I felt like joining in.

"I can make you a copy if you like," said Mark, feeling it too.

"Cheers mate, nice one," I said, beginning to think just I've found a new best mate.

"OK lovebirds, who fancies going to the shop, it's so hot, let's get a drink," said Cerys, standing up stretching her curves.

"OK," said Mark and me in unison.

Cerys sniggered and started walking. I was just about to fall into place next to her when Mark cut in front of me, put his arm around her waist and I thought oh yeah, oh what? Oh, fuck!!! I fell into line behind them with Gobber at my side, slowly but surely my lip curled up into a snarl at the sight of them cuddling up, nuzzling, whispering in each other's ears, occasionally laughing, playfully pushing one another. It felt wrong, so, very, very wrong. I thought fuck this, a copy of Donut 1 or not, I'm going to talk to her the first chance I get.

Mark offered to buy the drinks and disappeared into the shop with Gobber, leaving Cerys and me, on our own.

I thought the first chance I get: go, go, go.

"He's alright, he is," I opened with.

She smiled, "Yeah, he's a nice bloke... And a good laugh... He's a bit vain though."

I laughed, saw the opportunity, blundered in, "A bit vain, is he? I know you, you don't like vain blokes, come on Cerys, what is this?

176

You trying to make me jealous or what?"

"Huh… Don't flatter yourself, Skinner, if you want to go out with your mates, smashing stuff up, causing trouble, that's up to you. I've got other plans."

"Oh yeah, like there's so much to do around here, isn't there? There's nothing, only Joey Deacon work, and even that's hard to find and if you're unlucky enough to get it, the wages are shit, it's not worth it. Thatcher's fucked this country, and we're the end product."

Cerys snorted, "I'm not going to give up, even if you have. I'm going to college to re-do my O Levels and if I passed them, I'm going to do my nurse training, be a RGN. I'm going to do something meaningful with my life, not just waste it away."

"Oh well done, yeah let's get qualified, work on an old people's ward wiping shitty arses and get paid pennies for doing it," I said, raising my voice.

"Oh, shut up, Skinner, there's something wrong with you."

Mark came back out of the shop, killing the argument stone dead.

I thought I am doing something constructive with my life, and I'm going to prove it.

"Oi Mark, we've got a gig on Saturday night in Ware, if you're interested."

"Yeah, definitely," said Mark, without even thinking about it.

I looked to Cerys.

177

"Yeah, we'll be there," she said, in a tone of reconciliation.

"Where is it?" Mark asked, giving himself a once over in the reflection of the shop window.

Chapter 10

Karen Corker

On the night before our next gig at, The Founder's Hall, Andy, Whiff and me were sitting in the window seats in The Tap, having a few pints, just generally watching the world go by, when Whiff saw a girl he knew, walking past with a group of mates. Whiff leant forwards, banged on the window, waving madly at her, she reciprocated, giving him a big smile, mouthing 'Whiffy' joyously, blowing a kiss in his direction.

"Penneeee, I'm going to go and say hello," said Whiff standing up, running out leaving his smouldering roll up in the ashtray.

Andy smirked, "You know who that is, don't you?"

"Nah mate, is it another Whiff woman, one of the harem?" I asked, grinning.

Andy laughed, "I don't know, probably."

"No, it's Penny, you know… she's like a man."

"Oh, that Penny," I said, smiling.

Whiff had told us about a girl he had been chatting up called Penny, he'd said that he wanted to go out with her, as she was into good music, drank pints, and you could have a proper conversation with her 'like she was a man'. Instantly 'is she like a man' became the catchphrase of the week for the band, if Whiff happened to mention anyone female, even his mum, the reply would always be 'is she like a man?'

Andy and me sat back, watching Whiff and Penny chatting.

"I wonder if they're talking about motors," I suggested.

Andy laughed and volunteered, "Pigeon fancying?"

Whiff strolled back in looking animated.

"Is she still like a man?" Andy asked, sending us both into fits of laughter.

"What were you talking about? Football?"

"Combustion engines?" Andy added.

Whiff picked up his roll up looking confused, "Oh ha… Ha peasants," he said, eventually catching on.

"You know what, Whiff, you've got really strange taste in girls," I said.

"What do you mean?" He asked, puffing away.

"You like them to be men."

Whiff laughed and drawled, "Ware; where the men are men and the women are men." He picked up his pint and downed half of it, wiping the froth off his top lip, "Pen, reckons there's a party up King's Hill tonight, and she might be able to get us in."

I smiled, nodding my head, "Yeah, sounds good mate"

180

"I like a party, maybe we can top up a few pints again?" I suggested, smirking.

Whiff shook his head, "I'm not doing that again. I'm going to behave myself."

I studied him for a moment, "Bollocksss," I said, not believing a word of it.

Whiff shrugged and sunk the rest of his pint, banging it down onto the solid wood table.

"Is it a man-only party?" Andy joked.

Whiff belched towards Andy. "Well, if it is, you won't be allowed in Andrew," said Whiff, already walking to the door.

"Oi hold up, man," I said, before sinking the rest of my pint.

"Come on, mate," I said to Andy over my shoulder, following Whiff through the open door.

"I'm not an alcoholic, like you two," Andy said, taking his time, finishing his pint.

A warm breeze greeted us on Ware High Street, I took my leather jacket off, slung it over my shoulder, Andy and Whiff both doing the same.

Penny and her mates pulled away from us on the straight, passing The Cannon's hotel, the park at Cannon's Drive; Kings Hill glinting in the distance in front of them.

Whiff said, "Come on, we need to catch up, we won't get in without her," lagging well behind us.

"Well moooooove then Whifters," I Alan-ed, over my shoulder.

"Yeah, hurry up, lardy," Andy instructed.

"Piss off, chipmunk," Whiff counter instructed.

Penny and her mates left the A10, went up the hill that the Kings Hill estate was named after and up onto the Kings Hill estate itself. By the time we got there, we could already hear the steady boom of a bass drum phasing in and out, as it bounced off the nearby shops and houses.

"We need to catch her up, or we won't get in," Whiff repeated.

"She's too fast. She walks like a man," Andy laughed.

I crooned, "She walks like a man, my son." In falsetto.

Whiff rolled his eyes, looking like he'd had enough of that one.

Penny turned onto Heath Drive, congregating with some more of her mates, outside a semi-detached house that had every light in every room switched on, waiting for us to catch up. Whiff strolled over to her, gave her a cuddle, they talked for a while, then he nodded for us to follow them up a short path to the white UPVC front door.

Penny rang the bell, the three of us silently took cover, falling in behind her mates.

A moment later, an elegantly dressed girl opened the door, a big smile spread across her heavily made-up face.

"Hiya Pen, you've had your haircut. It really suits you, very waif like, I love it, it suits you."

"It's like a man," I whispered to Andy, who stifled a laugh, trying to remain anonymous in amongst Penny's mates.

"Come in, come in," Our host gushed.

Penny stepped over the threshold, followed by her mates.

One by one our host greeted...

"Oh hello, Jack."

"Hello, Liam."

"Hi, Abbie."

"Nice to see you, Jess."

"Come in Sue."

I held back and then when one of the fatter ones made for the entrance, I nuzzled up with her more than ample arse cheeks and slipped into the party unseen.

A huge group of people jammed up the hallway, which was made worse by the big bum in front of me, so I turned to see how the others were fairing.

"Hi Sally, this is Whiff… He's in the year above us at Fanshawe, you know him?" Penny asked.

"Oh yes, I've seen you about, nice to meet you Whiff," Sally replied and Whiff smiled angelically like an altar boy.

While Penny, Sally and Whiff chatted away, Andy saw his chance, ducked into the hallway next to me, looking down at the heifer sized arse in front of us, grimacing.

"If she farts now, it'll either cause a stampede or it will bring the fucking walls down," I mumbled into Andy's ear.

Andy snorted, snorted again and the arse's owner spun around, so we quickly about faced, pretending to see how Whiff was getting on. I had never seen Whiff being so pleasant before, he was all sweetness and light, not only was it hilarious, if you didn't know him, you'd have thought that he was a complete gentleman. Once Whiff had charmed our host into submission, got himself in, the log jam eased, and we made our way into the front room to find a party in full swing.

I had never seen so many people in such a small area, there must have been forty party goers, drinking, dancing, laughing, chatting. In one corner of the room a black stack system thumped out dance music, in the other, mountains of lager, various bottles of wine and spirits teetered up dangerously towards the ceiling, the pilers almost bouncing along with the music. On a table next to us there was a treasure trove of snacks; sandwiches, crisps, sweets, Vol-Au-Vents, cheese on sticks, sausages on sticks, fruit on sticks, loads of stuff on sticks, that some hungry party goers were feasting on.

I smiled broadly at Andy, "Come on then, let's get stuck in."

Andy smiled, grabbed the nearest tin, pulled the tab, "Here's to our generous host… Er what's her name again?"

I grabbed one myself, "Fucked if I know."

Andy proclaimed, "Here's to- fucked if I know!"

Whiff repeated, "To fucked if I know," downing the tin in one go, then he ostentatiously crushed the can in his hand and dropped it to the floor.

A few snakebites later, and once again the shit music wasn't an issue anymore, in fact I was feeling a lot better about the world in general, even the thought of Cerys cuddling up, nuzzling, playfully pushing Mark didn't bother me anymore. I was relaxed, sat back, swigging another pint of the sweet amnesia juice taking the rowdy room in, when I noticed Lee's old girlfriend Karen and Lucy 'flat' Chesterman were standing in the corner, near beer mountain talking with a group of girls. Karen had changed since I had seen her at our gig at Thundridge youth club; gone were the skinhead boots, braces and clipped hair of a skin girl. Now it was a tight-fitting black dress, six-inch heels and luscious dark ringlets of brown hair, I thought she looked absolutely stunning. A smiling Lucy caught me peeping over and nudged Karen, who smiled, pointing over in my direction, her index beckoning me over.

I pointed at myself stupidly as if to say who me? Lil' ole me? They both fell into each other, cracking up laughing.

"Andy, can you keep Whiff occupied, I'm er… going over there," I said, walking away before he could answer.

"Oooh Skinner, you haven't changed a bit," Karen said, checking my black bondage trousers with white zips, as I sauntered up to the group.

I smiled. "You have," I said, suggestively, instantly regretting it.

Lucy laughed, "You better watch out Kaz, this one's trouble"

"I know he is Lucy, I used to talk to him when I was going out with Lee, you remember?"

"Oh, Lee was lovely, how could you chuck him?" Lucy said.

Karen cackled mischievously.

"You OK Lucy, you saw Toyah last week, didn't you?" I asked her.

"Yeah, she was brilliant, thanks, her hair is amazing."

"Your band's good Skinner, Virus V1, cool name," said Karen, her dark eyes zoning in on me.

"Cheers," I said, feeling embarrassed.

"Stand up protest, don't argue," shouted Karen, putting her fist up.

I creased up; it was close enough.

"You haven't changed much either Karen, still a hooligan, I remember you around the village when you were younger, with your boots and braces singing all those two-tone tracks."

"Oh yeah, and you told me that you liked some of Madness' songs and made me promise not to tell anyone," said Karen laughing, brushing her new locks away from her eyes.

"Night boat to Cairo, you know I used to fancy you," I said, smiling broadly.

"Yeah, I knew, a girl knows these things, I fancied you too," she said, confidently leaning in, her nose almost touching mine.

"I think I'm going to go now," said Lucy, backing away.

"OK, Lucy flat Chesterman," said Karen, creasing up.

Lucy said, "Oi, not anymore," pushing her boobs up.

"Ooooh, not bad," said Karen, giving them a gentle squeeze.

Karen and Lucy fell about laughing, then Lucy gave us a sad little wave goodbye and headed for the rapidly deteriorating mountain of beer.

I waved back, "See you, Lucy."

"Now she's definitely changed, she's Lucy fat Chesterman now," I proclaimed.

Karen fell forward into fits of laughter. "Chicken fillets," she said, wiping at her eyes.

"What?"

"She's got chicken fillets in her bra, it's like a push-up bra. Unlike mine, mine are all real," she told me, putting her hands underneath her huge breasts, pushing them up for me to inspect.

"Oh yeah," I said as causally I could, running my eyes over her extensive cleavage.

I thought fucking hell, I'm having another Mrs. Gates moment here, only this time, I know exactly what they are and what they are for.

I resisted the impulse to pull at my groin, even though my fast-growing hard on, was getting caught up in the elastic of my boxer shorts.

Karen pinned me with her dark tractor beam eyes, "Where were we? Oh yeah, you used to fancy me when I was going out with Lee, didn't you Skinner?"

"Yeah, you were alright for a skin girl…" I said coolly, trying to ignore the hard on pushing up in my trousers like a tent pole.

I hope she doesn't look down. I thought.

"I used to wonder what would have happened if Lee and Clare hadn't been around," Karen said, her eyes still burning into me.

I moved forward, she smiled as my hard on brushed her stomach, I grinned back helplessly, put my arms around her waist and whispered into her ear, "Yeah, me too. We could have gone fishing, had a picnic or done a bit of birdwatching."

She laughed, pushing me away playfully.

I looked into her eyes, smiling broadly, "Clare and Lee aren't here now… What shall we do?"

Karen eyes glanced over towards the stairs that led to the bedrooms, I followed her eyes.

"Oh yeah? Come on then, let's do some birdwatching," I suggested with a hopefully, winning smile.

"Hmm, yeah, let's have a picnic," she laughed back at my winning smile.

Whiff and Andy came piling down the stairs, indiscriminately barging people out the way. I thought fuck off, fuck off, fuck off, fuck off, fuck off, fuck off. Whiff gave me a cursory nod, Andy waved minutely, and they began pushing their way through the dancers in front of the stereo system towards the door. I looked at them closely, not only was their hair wet, both seemed to be covered in a white powder, which could have only been talc. Fuck off. Fuck off, fuck off, fuck off, fuck off, I thought, all over again, and seeing that they actually were, I returned my attention to the lovely Karen.

"Skinner, are you OK; you look like you've just seen a ghost?"

"I'm fine Karen, come here," I said, gently pulling her forward, kissing her on her full purple lips. Immediately, she responded by opening her mouth, putting her tongue into mine.

I took her hand, and we slowly glided towards the stairs, grinning at each other, like newly-weds.

Lucy and a group of five or six girls cut across, in front of us, blocking our route.

189

"Hey, hey, where do you think you're going?" Asked Lucy, placing her hand on Karen's arm, like an arresting officer.

"Oh no you don't Karen, come on, let's get some more drinks," chided another girl, taking her other arm.

I thought, fuck off, fuck off, fuck… Oh, and watched Karen walk away with her capturers, she turned, blew me a kiss, then disappeared into the clutch of dancers in front of the stereo.

Oh fuck, oh fuck, oh fuck ohhhhhhhh fuuuuucccckkk, I thought, I was angry, frustrated confused. I only knew one thing now, the massive hard on I had only a moment ago, was now wilting, rescinding, dying, only to be replaced by the nagging urge to piss out the by-product of the four pints of snakebite that were sloshing about down there in the same area.

'I Want to be Free' by Toyah followed me out of the lounge, I turned at the door, Lucy, Karen and the other girls danced, gyrating their hips, putting their glasses to their lips, drinking the sweet wine, Karen saw me and waved extravagantly only to disappear again in the dancing throng.

Once in the bathroom, I pissed out a couple of pints of liquid into the cistern from my now limp, last turkey in the shop like, dick, gave the loose skin a quick shake, zipped up and left for the kitchen, where I grabbed a can of cider off one of the work tops, to go back into the lounge with. On my way out, I bumped into Danny, almost spilling his drink.

"You alright Danny? Good party, yeah?" I said, noticing his stoned red eyes.

190

"Indeed, it is, my man, indeed it is. I'm fucking wasted. I saw Ashley last night, we went up The Frontline, got some great sensi," he beamed.

"Oh yeah, nice one, so you skinning up any time soon?"

Danny laughed, grabbing a couple of cans himself, "I don't need to, Skinner; Brother Vincent should be putting one together as we speak."

"Oh, nice one, lead the way," I grinned like a man who had just lost everything on a dice roll, only to win the lottery the very next day. "So how is your little disciple these days?" I shouted as we wiggled our way through the groups of dancers in the lounge.

Danny laughed, traversing the heifer's arse as it wobbled to the sounds of Toyah, "He's still learning from the master."

"Huh, master bater more like," I returned.

"Is he still a boring twat? I mean, has he actually said anything today?" I asked.

Danny smiled knowingly, nodding his head along to the music, and we fell into single file at the bottom of the stairs. Danny took the lead as we paced up, and I noticed more of the white powder on the carpet, there was also a sticky white and blue substance on the railing.

On the landing, a woman was down on her hands and knees, sweeping at the powder that was deeply entrenched in the carpet pile, her face red and angry, above her two big blokes stood, arms

191

folded, fists balled who looked up as we passed, nailing us both with accusing stares. Danny looked away, ignoring them, made his way to a room at the end of the landing, and we entered. Inside, underneath huge clouds of marijuana smoke, I could see four or five groups of people sitting in circles passing spliffs around, at the back under a window sat Brother Vincent, cradling a small bong in his hands, like a mother with a newly born.

"Ah, grasshopper, you have done well," Danny said, snatching the small glass device from his possessive arms.

Brother Vincent smiled vacantly, watching his treasure go.

I hadn't smoked a bong before, but judging by the state of Danny's eyes and the general state of Brother 'sweat dreams' Vincent, I was in for a treat. Danny flipped the ash from the bong into an empty pint glass and began topping the silver bowl up with fresh sensi from The Frontline.

"What was that on the stairs, Danny?" I asked.

"Oh yeah man, it was your mates Andy and Whiff, they went mental in the bathroom, chucking stuff everywhere, Sally's brothers are going to kill them the next time they see them," said Danny, patting the herb into the bowl.

I laughed and shook my head sadly. I thought oh yeah Whiff you're going to behave yourself this time, oh well at least you didn't fuck it up with Karen, I did that for myself.

Danny sparked his lighter, put it to the bowl, the flame crackling hungrily at the grass, he took a huge lung full, grinned lopsidedly, blowing out a huge nimbus of white smoke and slowly laid back onto a girl sitting behind him.

"Oh, sorry," he said, grinning at her.

I rolled my eyes at her, and she smiled peacefully back at us.

"What were you doing sniffing around Karen Corker, Skinner? Lee still fancies her," Danny warned from his now horizontal position.

I thought, oh what, that's her second name! Whiff would have had a field day with that one, quite rightly too, as Karen is.

I snorted, "Oh yeah? I reckon she's moved on, mate."

"Why aren't you down there with her then?"

I smiled wistfully, "It's sad man, don't laugh but, her mates saved her from me."

Danny laughed, "Oh no bad one, saved by the cavalry, was she?"

I creased up at the thought of her mates coming over the horizon like the cavalry, to save her from my evil clutches.

"Oh well, fuck her," I proclaimed, "I'm getting off with Mary Jane tonight." Picking up the bong

"Oh, sorry mate, where's my manners, you want to go next Vincent?" I asked, stopping.

"Hmm…" said Brother Vincent.

"Yeah, No?" I asked again, unsure what 'Hmm' meant.

"Hmm…" echoed Brother Vincent.

"Yes, No? Definitely, maybe?" I said, beginning to lose my patience.

"Yeah, no yeah I, er, hmm…" said Brother Vincent wrestling with the question like his answer might change the whole future of mankind.

"I'm sorry Danny, but your mate is fucking weird, why doesn't he say anything? I'm not going to fucking bite, you know," I stated, not caring that he was listening.

"Hmm…" Danny Vincent-ed back, in fits of laughter.

"Hello, hello, Earth calling Brother Vincent, come in, do you read me?" I said, smirking.

"Oh, he's alright, aren't you, Vincent?"

"Hmmm…" said Brother Vincent, looking down, his face reddening.

I sighed at the bloke, took the bong from Danny, fired it up, filling my lungs with the sweet flowery incense, and at once I felt the warm cradling effects spread through my body,

"Ah that's some good sensi Danny. Isn't it Vincent?" I asked.

"Yeah, yeah, yeah," he simpered back, his head nodding wildly, like his neck was made of string.

I thought wow, progress and immediately took another couple of hits from the bong to celebrate my breakthrough.

A mellow feeling smoothly caressed me and I thought nah he's alright, leave him alone, so at peace in my time, I laid down next to Danny who was finding the ceiling very interesting.

"It's waving Skinner, look, look," he said, pointing up.

"Oh yeah," I said, seeing a shadow of a hand projected up onto the ceiling by an ornamental lamp next to a large four-poster bed at the head of the room.

"It's waving my brain goodbye," Danny joked.

"What brain?" I returned.

Danny creased up, stretching out his arms, getting more comfortable.

A moment later, Brother Vincent said, "Yeah…"

I craned my neck forwards, viewing him.

"Is he taking the fucking piss Danny?"

"No, he's alright aren't you Vincent, you're just quiet, aren't you?"

Brother Vincent smiled self-consciously in our direction, then nodded, looking back down at the carpet, and I reached for the bong again, groaning inwardly…

A couple of decent lung fills later, I was back slabbed out next to Danny.

"So, what happened earlier with Whiff and Andy?"

"I don't really know, you saw it, didn't you, Vincent?"

Oh, for fucks sake, I thought, sighed deeply and asked, "Did you see it, Vincent?" I interrogated him, thinking you bastard, you're wasting time, my precious, precious time.

"Yeah," he said.

"What happened then?"

"Hmmmmmmm… I don't… hmm…"

"You saw what happened, yeah…? Did you see it happen?" I asked angrily, as peace in my time slowly evaporated, into the invasion of Poland.

"Yeah, yeah…" He trailed off.

"Oh, for fucks sake, it's like one of life's constants, isn't it? Tides change, seasons change, life changes, everything except you Brother Vincent, you are the one constant, we all know you'll be out there, boring everyone to death," I said insightfully, feeling like I had said something profound, full of meaning, and in the process put the balance right.

Danny saw it too, cracking up laughing, "I reckon that just about sums you up doesn't it, Brother Vincent?"

196

"Yeah, hmmmmm," he burbled self-consciously, reddening even more at the cheeks.

I wanted to punch the little knob end, thinking maybe it would loosen up his tongue a bit, maybe he might venture an opinion, say something, anything, call me a wanker, even ouch would have been something, but instead I lay back down, feeling the soporific pollen of the sensimelia inside, gently washing through me and got back to the undulating ceiling.

Danny's waving hand had turned into a multitude of waving hands slowly waving me off into a pleasant doze, so I stretched out, drifting off into a gentle sleep.

I woke up with a start, where am I? Oh yeah, the party, the music had stopped, the house was totally silent apart from a deep rasping sound as Danny slept beside me. I focused in on my surroundings, as my eyes became accustomed to the light, looking beyond Danny, spread out across the room, people were curled up, laying pod like in sleeping bags.

In the middle of the bedroom, someone had made themselves comfortable in the large four-poster bed, stretching out self-indulgently, making the soft sheets quiver.

A moment later the door flew open, flooding the room with light, in walked Karen, fag in one hand, a bottle of wine in the other.

"Whey, hey, what's going on in here then?"

"Skinner? Is that you?" She asked, bending forwards, furrowing her brow.

197

"Yeah, yeah you alright, Karen?" I replied, drowsily.

"Oh, where did you go, I've been looking for you, my friends said I should keep away from you, they say I'm on the rebound, I ditched them though, what do they know, they're no fun," she said, beaming at me, taking me into her confidence.

"Please, please, turn the light off will you! I'm trying to sleep here!" A bloke in one of the sleeping bags protested grumpily.

"Oh, sorry Pete, is this the sleeping room?" She whispered drunkenly, raising her voice.

"Yes," Pete stated coldly.

Karen Corker stubbed out her fag on the Goblin Teasmade next to the bed, laughing to herself.

"OK Pete, I'm going to bed then," she declared, unzipping her blueberry-coloured dress, which slid to the floor, revealing a stacked black bra and tight panties.

"Owwwwwh," groaned Pete, watching her.

An amused Karen looked around the dark room, twanged her bra strap twice, grinned, shrugged her shoulders, reached behind herself, and her bra fell away revealing her full white breasts.

"Owwwhhhh," came from another sleeping bag near the door.

"Ooooowwhhh, bloody hell," said Pete, not interested in sleeping any more.

Karen giggled, rolled her tight black knickers off and slipped under the sheets of the bed.

"Oh, sorry," she said, finding the bed occupied.

"It's fine, there's plenty of room, I'll budge up," said another girl's voice full of laughter.

"Oh, my," said Pete, summing up the collective feeling of every bloke in the room.

I heard another moan from the sleeping bag near the door, and listened as Karen and the other girl stretched out luxuriously, the bed squeaking as it bore their combined weight.

OK, no matter what I do, I thought, I'm going to try to get into that bed, because if I don't, I might not regret it today in this haze, but I'll regret for the rest of my life. Now, how am I going to do that without either looking like a right prat, or worse still a fucking rapist?

"You alright, Karen?" I asked.

"Yeeaaahhh," she sang, the bed creaking softly under her.

"Is it warm in there?" I asked, now beginning to feel like a prat. "It's cold out here." Being a total prat.

Pete complained, "Oh Jesus," under his breath, agreeing with my synopsis.

I thought to myself, stop being such a wanker, get into the bed with them; I know what's the best that can happen, surely that far outweighs the worst, doesn't it?

I steeled myself, breaking cover and tip toed over to the bed.

"I need a warm-up," I said, with as much confidence as I could muster.

Karen pulled the blankets back, "Come on in then," she gestured.

I triumphantly rolled in next to her, she snuggled up close, kissing my neck and began rubbing my chest. I had waited long enough now and was powerless to stop my hands reaching around and cupping her beautiful breasts, which felt soft and yielding to my touch.

"I've seen you looking at them all night, you like them don't you Skinner, they're bigger than Clare's, aren't they?" She whispered.

"I'm not sure, give us a minute," I said, giving them a squeeze.

"OK, that's enough for me, I'm off," said the other bed dweller.

Karen and me cracked up laughing, watching the girl evacuate our bed, then once she was out and settled on the floor, Karen arched her back, pushing my hand down between her legs, showing me where she really liked to be touched. I moved my fingers up and down in the vicinity of her clitoris, her hand grabbing hungrily at my cock, rubbing it through my bondage trousers.

"Let's get these off," she whispered.

Karen pulled at the button, deftly freeing it and unzipped my fly, easing them down only for one of my bondage straps to get snagged around my foot.

I laughed, "Houston, we have a problem."

Karen giggled, "What are you like? Let me do that."

Karen ducked her head down under the blankets in pursuit of the errant bondage strap, her smooth cheek slid over my granite hard dick on the way. I thought I was going to cum there and then, so I projected images of dead kittens, The Soup Dragon's scowling face and the look on Pete O'Shea's face when he had shat in Olaf's sleeping bag onto my rampant, rampaging, ready to pop mind.

A moment later my bondage trousers slid onto the floor and as she came up, her luscious hair ran over my cock, sending me into delirium.

Nick, Nick there is shit in my sleeping bag I thought, replaying the hapless German's cries for help, crisis averted, I gently began to finger her moist fanny. Karen arched her back again for maximum stimulation, groaning with delight.

"I'm on the pill, let's do it, Skinner."

A door opened, followed by a blinding light as the bedroom light switched on, through my stinging eyes I saw a big bloke with a neck like a bulldog appear from behind the bedroom door, his face going from disbelief to absolute rage in the blink of my stoned eyelid.

"WHAT THE FUCK ARE YOU TWO DOING IN MY FUCKING BED? GET OUT NOW!" He bellowed, pointing a podgy finger in our direction, then gaped, "Bloody hell Karen not you again, go downstairs and see Sally and you Sid Vicious get out of my fucking bed before I drag you out, I know you and your mates gate crashed."

"OK, OK, keep your hair on mate, I'm going."

I pulled back the duvet, revealing my engorged red, angry dick for all to see.

"Euuugh," came from Pete, sniggering came from the sleeping bag near the door.

"Ahhh, no, no, no, put some fucking clothes on, put some clothes on, will you!?" Bulldog ordered, putting his hands in front of his eyes.

"I don't know what's happened to you over the last couple of years Karen, believe me, I will be talking to your mum this time," said Bulldog neck from behind his hands.

"Huh, like she cares, the old cow," Karen spat.

"Karen, believe me she does... look, I'm not getting into this with you now."

Once we were both dressed, out of the bed, Bulldog neck disgustedly pulled the duvet and under sheets off, chucking then to the floor and marched me towards the door.

"Oh yeah, if there's anyone else here who isn't a friend of Sally, then I would strongly advise that you get out now."

I blew a sad kiss at Karen, kicking Danny's silent sleeping bag as I wandered past.

"See you later friends of Sally," I drawled, "See you soon, Karen."

"Yeah, soon, Skinner," she said, waving sadly.

"Skinner! Huh, what kind of name is that? Come on then, Skinner, let's go."

I followed Bulldog neck's big frame out of the door, down the stairs, where we passed a woman on her knees, kitchen scourer in her hand, still furiously trying to remove white powder from the stair carpet, despite her best efforts it wasn't going well, if anything she was making it worse.

"It's a fucking liberty, you have a party for your daughter and little bastards like this show up and think it's funny to ruin the house," Bulldog neck spat.

"Yes," said the woman distractedly.

"I'll tell you now, mate, I had nothing to do with that."

"Oh yeah, we'll see," said Bulldog, leading me into the lounge.

Whiff and Andy were standing in one corner near the stereo and about ten blokes, armed with pool cues, baseball bats and other heavy objects were standing in the other glaring at them. I knew what had happened, I also knew that in their eyes I was guilty by association, so I trudged over to stand with my mates. I had no choice; I knew they'd do the same for me.

Bulldog broke the silence, "OK let's all calm down now, it's Sally's birthday. I don't want it ending like this."

"Oh, come on Gary, you seen the mess they made in the bathroom, punks by name punks by nature, fucking punks," said a bloke wearing a Pringle shirt, pointing a Kirk Stevens two-piece cue at us.

"Pat I would love to, believe me, it's Sally's day though, it's not ending like this."

Bulldog slowly turned towards us, "OK listen up punks, you better get out of here before I change my mind, go on the three of you get out and thank your lucky stars that I don't set this lot on you, because they'd eat your fucking livers."

I thought yep, I reckon that's our cue to leave, so I made my way to the door with the other two following close behind, and we got the hell out of there, quick time.

Once we had got off the King's Hill estate, feeling a bit safer, we stopped for a roll up.

"OK, go on then what happened?" I asked, pulling hard on my roll up.

"It was classic, Skin," said Whiff, grinning from ear to ear.

Andy said, "Whiffy here told me he could see my house from the bathroom window."

"And when he leant out of the window to look, I filled his hair up with Colgate extra bright, sniff his hair, go on, you'll see," said a grinning Whiff cutting in.

I cracked up, took a sniff and I must admit it did have a minty freshness about it,

"OK, and then what?" I asked.

"I couldn't let that go, so I have him a good talc-ing," said Andy proudly.

Whiff creased up, "Perfume, soap, shampoo, conditioner towels shaving foam flannels everything got chucked."

"Yeah, we must have been the best smelling vandals in history," quipped Andy, in fits of laughter.

I cackled at the over perfumed punk rockers, "I saw you two coming down the stairs covered in talc."

"Oh yeah," said Whiff, "You were with the Corker."

"Oh what, you know her?"

"Yeah, she's well known around Ware, Skin."

"Oh, what, is she?" I said, disappointedly.

"Yeah but that doesn't mean anything, I like her she's a good laugh, likes a drink, and you can talk to her too," Whiff said, trying to make me feel better.

"Is she like a man?" A smiling Andy asked.

"Nah, Andy, she's nothing like a man" I assured him.

Whiff, Andy and me got up and began the walk back to Andy's house.

"I have to know this, why the fuck did you come back?"

"I was beginning to ask the same question myself," Whiff said, scratching at his dark stubble,

"We came back to see if you were OK, and that's when all those uggers turned up."

I sighed, slapping my forehead continuously. "I was fine, fine, fine, oh fuck me I was fine," I cried.

"I bet you were Skin," said Whiff, understanding. "Corker, Corker, Corker. Corker, Corker, Corker," he chanted.

Once we had safely made it to Andy's house, Andy tiptoed up the path, hoping not to disturb his sleeping parents.

As he opened the door, I said, "Oi Andy, don't forget to brush your teeth mate."

Andy put his hand up to his head, pinged a slither of white paste out from behind his ear with his finger and began to rub his teeth with it, creasing up into manic laughter.

"See you tomorrow, Andy," I called out.

Andy's front door clicked shut, and I pulled a spliff I had cadged from Danny earlier on from my jacket pocket, holding it under Whiff's nose

"Taa dah!" I said, like Tommy Cooper getting a trick right for once.

Whiff's ultra-white teeth grinned back at me in the darkness. "Yeesss," he said like a pool's winner.

I dextrously flipped it up into my mouth and dived into my pocket for my lighter.

"Nah, not here, Skin… let's find somewhere out of the way, it's too dodgy," Whiff said.

"OK, how about down by the river, then?" I said, disappointedly slipping it back into my pocket.

"Yeah, good idea," he returned.

Whiff and me turned down New Road towards the river.

"I'll tell you what Skin, I'll show you Founder's Hall on the way."

I laughed, slapping my head theatrically, "Oh yeah, the gig, fucking hell."

"Oh well, we'll be knackered, but Dave and Andy won't be, they'll carry us," Whiff said.

I sniggered, "Nah, Dave's staying around Steph's again tonight, I doubt he'll be getting much sleep, she'll be chucking him around the bedroom all night long."

Whiff laughed, "Oh yeah, she's a right goer that Steph, isn't she? Nice too, what a jammy bastard."

"Yeah, she is mate," I said, nodding wistfully, thinking of what Karen Corker and me could be doing right now.

"You know, Dave actually asks for my advice about girls sometimes."

Whiff snorted, "Why on earth would he do that?"

"I haven't got a clue, mate, it's like asking Enoch fucking Powell for tips on Jamaican cooking."

Whiff stopped and pointed, "Here we are Skin there it is, Founder's Hall, our next gig."

I walked up to it, checking it out. It's a decent-sized venue I thought, about the same size as Thundridge Village Hall, should fit a few people in tonight. I moved in closer and saw that, in fact, it was exactly the same as Thundridge Village Hall, it had the same pebble dashed concrete outer shell and the same white plinth with its date of completion written on it sitting above its entrance; two light brown double doors.

"It could be good this one. Andy said it's another CND benefit. He reckons they'll be a few in tonight," I said, enthusiastically.

"Nah… It's not CND," Whiff said, "I was there when he arranged it. Did he say that?"

"Yeah, he said Necro did one here a while back."

Whiff shook his head, "Nah, I don't think so, Skin, not this one anyway."

"Oh, OK," I said, disappointedly, walking up to the glass notice board to the left of the main entrance.

I put my hand up to shield my eyes from the glare of the street lights and I read from top to bottom

Jazzer-size, with Jason and Jenny.
Monday's, Wednesday's, Friday's, 10am

Badminton.
Thursday Nights, 7pm onwards.

The Late, Late, Breakfast Club, Wednesdays, 3pm till 7pm.

Don's Cleaning Services,
Any time, Any place, Anywhere!
In the Ware area.

"Oh well, at least he's got a flyer up," I said, seeing a card blue-tacked onto the top of the glass.

"Come on, let's go down the river and have that smoke," Whiff suggested.

"Yeah, good idea. It's sensiiii time."

Whiff and me strolled along Church Street under a jewel encrusted sky, passing the back of the church, the moon above the steeple, shining on us like it was showing us the way, and we came up to the boarded-up school of St Mary's Juniors.

I stopped outside the locked gates, "Whoa hold up Whiff. I've got an idea."

I peeked left then right, saw the coast was clear, vaulted over the gates, ambled round the back of the school, leaving Whiff's protests behind me, lost in the still night air.

In the playground at the back of the school, darkness folded in around me like a blanket, away from the streetlights. Inside the gloom I could just about make out a boarded-up window. I thought that will do, grabbed a discarded four-by-two out of a nearby builder's skip, slipped it behind the board and attempted to jemmy it open. A couple of hard thrusts and the board toppled backwards, missing me by an inch, dropping to the ground with an almighty crash.

Whiff came running around the back. "Skin, Skin, there's a car coming," he said, out of breath.

"Whiff, you worry too much, man."

In a second, the car swept harmlessly past the front of the school and away into the night.

I climbed into the window and Whiff scrabbled up, following reluctantly.

Inside it was cave-like, silent, damp, apart from the odd stab of light from the streetlights coming in through the boards that were covering the windows up, it was pitch black.

Whiff and me stumbled, blindly through the darkness, arms stretched out in front of us, kicking into various discarded objects on the floor, eventually coming into the old assembly hall.

In through two oval shaped windows at the far end of the hall, shone an ethereal light, illuminating more detritus, chairs, tables and building materials that lay strewn all around us. I picked a battered chair up off the dusty floor, launched it as hard as I could against a wall, sending shockwaves, echoing off throughout the building.

"Skin don't do that, you'll get us nicked," said Whiff running to the window, nervously peeping out. "Skin I know you'll think I'm bullshitting, but there's a copper on the High Street, and he's looking this way," his voice quaking with fear.

I laughed, "You're right, I don't believe you, that's because you are bullshitting, my friend."

"Seriously, there's a copper on the high street!"

"Oi, you," I shouted in my best Ian Simms impression.

"Oi, did you touch my records? That's theft, that is."

Whiff stifled a laugh, I walked over to the window to take a look for myself, and it was true, a copper was strolling along the high street.

I pointed. "See that copper, he's come for you, you're going to jail you are," I Ian-ed faultlessly.

Whiff couldn't hold it any longer and threw his head back, laughing wholeheartedly, "Oi you," Whiff Ian- ed back at me.

"I'm going to get you, I am," said Whiff, falling into a heap, he was laughing so much.

I shouted, "WANKER!" at the top of my voice.

Plod stopped, began looking around, confused, he looked, left, right, left, right, then unbelievably up to the starlit sky, into the heaven's, above his tit head.

"Yeah, it's god, he's calling you, a… a… A WANKER!"

Whiff laughed. "See that copper, I think he really is going to get us," he said holding his sides, belly laughing.

Plod's head was still spinning left to right, tilting up and down, ears honing in, trying to work out where the shouts were coming from.

I smirked at the clown, "My mum always said you should end on a song, join in if you know this little ditty."

"I'll sing you a song, and it won't take long, all coppers are bastards, I'll sing you another one just like the other one, all coppers are bastards."

Whiff joined in, "The third verse is the same as the first, all coppers are bastards, the fourth verse is just as worse, all coppers are bastards."

Plod, still clueless, slowly healed off, while we serenaded him with another rendition of all coppers were born out of wedlock. He plodded off down the High Street, his soundtrack echoing from somewhere in the vicinity of the church, and finally the fool

212

disappeared from view. A few minutes of rolling around on the floor laughing later, I celebrated another victory by launching a dilapidated chair full power into the darkness and on contact, it shattered into a thousand pieces, sending another blast wave echoing into every corner of the school.

Whiff jumped back, holding his ears, as the sound faded away, into the open classrooms, both of us howling with laughter. Whiff snatched up a chair himself grinning at me, he chucked it, only it went upwards, instead of forwards and came crashing back down on him.

"You alright Whiff? I asked, as he brushed heaps of dust from his shoulders and hair.

"Yeah, I'm… oh shit it won't come off it's mixing with the shampoo from earlier," he said, dissolving into fits of laughter.

"This will make you feel better, Whiff."

"What?"

"Tah Dah," I said, flourishing the spliff from my pocket once more.

"That'll do nicely," he said, snatching it from my open hand.

Whiff and me, passed it between us, laughing, talking about the night, talking about the gig until we fell silent, eventually falling asleep as the early morning sun began to probe the oval windows, above our heads.

Chapter 11

Flounder's Hall

I woke up freezing cold, my body aching all over. I stretched out a limb that didn't seem to belong to me, it complained back, assuring me that it wished it didn't. In time, when I eventually dared to open my eyes, light surged in through the oval windows stabbing at my corneas, making my brain fizz like a well-used penny in a bottle of Rola Cola. I furiously rubbed at my sore peepers, trying to expel the Steradent like affect. It took a while.

Once I had shaken the snakebite blite off a bit, I took in my surroundings; saw broken chairs, smashed tables scattered all over the place, up above I saw the oval windows were of coloured glass, giving the small assembly hall a chapel like feel to it. I thought oh Jesus, Hilary would feel right at home here, quickly followed by, we've got to get out of this place. Now.

"Whiff mate, we need to get out of here right now," I said, giving his prone form a nudge.

"What? What? OK, yeah," he replied, drowsily.

Whiff opened his eyes, closed them again, opened them again.

"Oh, Jesus Christ, my fucking head Skin," he said, shakily getting onto his feet.

I sighed, "Tell me about it mate."

I started taking baby steps towards the door. Whiff and me gingerly dodged our way through our trail of mass of destruction; smashed

214

chairs, legless tables, ripped up floorboards, threw themselves up in front of us like an obstacle course, making us zigzag left then right to the exit and out. In the corridor, Whiff stopped and gaped into one of the silent classrooms, I moved up next to him, to see there was an effigy of a hanging man, in front of a scuffed blackboard, gently swinging to and fro the rope, creaking at its apex.

"Er… Whiff, did we do that?" I asked, nervously.

"No Skin, we didn't," came his reply.

"Let's get the fuck out here."

"Yeah, let's go back to mine," he agreed without hesitation.

Once we had clambered out of the school, we slowly trudged up the steep hill of Crib Street towards Whiff's house, my calves complaining all the way. I felt terrible. I didn't just feel like shit, I felt like the kind of shit that gets trodden on by crowds of people and then tromped up the road, leaving smudges all the way. To take my mind off my broken mind, my eyes sort out the new day dawning: the morning was beautiful.

A salient sun embraced the arrival of the new day in the east, pink clouds, embracing it, like they were wrapping it up, keeping it warm in the early morning chill. Whiff and me turned left at the top of Crib Street onto Milton Road, Whiff's road, and up to his house, number sixty-nine, then edged our way up the steep drive towards the front door.

Judy opened the door, before we even got near, face ashen, "Oh, Paul where have you been, I've been so worried."

"Ah don't worry, I was OK, we broke into St Mary's Juniors, crashed out on the floor in there didn't we Skin?" He said, laughing.

"Oh, Paul," Judy said, ushering us straight into the kitchen.

Inside the kitchen, it was welcoming, inviting, warm. I sighed and sat down heavily on a cushioned chair by the table, taking the weight off, rubbing at my aching thighs, calves, feet, head, while Judy fussed over us, pouring us orange juice, making tea, cooking beans, cutting up the bread and feeding the slices into the toaster like a hopeless gambler on a slot machine.

Whiff told her the full story of what had happened last night while she worked, which brought out a avalanche of 'Oh Paul's'. I was beginning to wonder when Whiff would have had enough of his mum's incessant fussing, when he inadvertently dropped a blob of butter onto his trousers and Judy moved in with the tablecloth, surely critical mass had been reached now.

"It's OK, it's OK, I'm doing it, I'm doing it," he said, bristling at the advancing cloth.

"Oh, Paul," she said, turning back to the sink.

I thought will he, or won't he say it?

"Silly old fucking bag," came my answer.

Judy gave him a final 'Oh Paul' and left him alone to eat his breakfast in peace.

Whiff and me ate in silence, our soundtrack the soporific hum of the fridge in the corner next to the other whites. When we were full, the

tiredness really came upon us, so we grabbed a couple of steaming
hot cups of tea and made our way up to his bedroom to crash out
for a while. A couple of roll ups and half the side of the Millions of
Dead Cops' album, I was drifting into a nice warm, cosy sleep. I was
nearly gone, nodding in my chair, when I heard the doorbell ring,
some doorstep chat and then, ominously, footsteps coming up the
stairs. Oh no, I thought feeling sorry for myself, I need to sleep and
as I raged at the injustice of this totally unwarranted, unwanted
intrusion, thinking things couldn't get any worse, Whiff's door opens
and David 'Custer' Cowley walks in.

David Cowley was one of the biggest posers in Ware. One day he
would be strutting along the high street in his bondage trousers with
his hair spiked up, the next he would be sitting in The Punch house,
a soul boy's pub, with his soul boy mates, hair coiffed, wearing
chinos and a Pringle top. In my mind, you were either a punk or you
weren't, you couldn't just change from day to day, it was a state of
mind, and once you entered into that state of mind, it was for keeps.
David Cowley was neither a punk nor a decent mate to Whiff, as far
as I was concerned, he was a shitter, someone who only looked after
number one.

Custer Cowley and Whiff had been jumped by an infamous local
skinhead gang, led by 'the unholy trinity' of Jamie Duggen, Stampy
and Glyn Mathews, at the back of Ware college, and without a single
thought for his mate, he had legged it, leaving Whiff to fight it out
on his own. Whiff had stood his ground, kicking out, throwing
punches at them, but in the end, there were just too many of them
and once they had got his big frame to the ground, they had gone in
hard with their DM's, sticking the boot in relentlessly, enjoying
themselves. Whiff had tried to protect himself by curling himself up
into a ball, the blows had still got through though, smashing his face
to a pulp and while those blows were falling, Custer had been in full

flight, leaving a brown trail of shit behind him as he legged it up Ware High Street. I couldn't believe it when Whiff told me that he bore him no malice whatsoever, he assured me that Cowley was alright, a good bloke. In fact, he reckoned that it was him who had been the sensible one, running away like that, he should've run off too. In a situation like that, I don't know what I would have done, but I knew one thing; I certainly wouldn't have left a mate to take a kicking like that on his own. Sometimes in life, you don't have a choice, you've just got to take a beating.

One of the skinheads, Jamie Duggan had been shot dead outside a pub in Watton-at-Stone, a few months after the attack on Whiff and although the newspapers had painted him as a misunderstood, lovable rogue and his Nan had said he was a 'little ray of sunlight' I thought good riddance, rest in piss you bastard, and maybe there is such a thing as karma after all.

Whiff and Cowley talked avidly about last night, in particular Whiff's chances of getting together with Penny, while I nodded in and out of sleep. David 'the Cowardly Custer' Cowley, as Andy and me called him, wasn't going to cut into my sleeping time; not only was I knackered, I thought, you've got to have some standards.

Whiff mentioned our gig tonight, while side two of the Millions of Dead Cops' album raged in the background. Cowley said he would be there; he knew a load of skins and punks he could ask; they said they would come down, and we would take the place over. I thought yeah, we'll see.

"Nice one, that would be brilliant, Dave," said Whiff, puffing on his fifth roll up of the day.

"I'm not just a pretty face mate, I know all the north London lot, I'll give them a tinkle, and they'll be well up for it," he said, confidently.

"Oh, good, I don't think many of the Thundridge lot will be coming, will they Skin?"

I snored in his direction, he grinned back, a bit embarrassed in front of his mate, then his face dropped off altogether as he heard the telltale soft footsteps on the stairs, alerting him that his mum was approaching, was she coming in? Of course, she was.

Whiff rolled his eyes to Custer as a smiling Judy walked in.

"Oh, hello, David," she chimed, happily.

"Hi Mrs. Hammersmith," he returned, pleasantly.

"Oh, Paul look at all this mess, I don't know how you manage, tsk, I just don't know......oh Paul," she said piling up, not only the cups we had taken up, but mould encrusted plates, a cracked tea pot and cutlery, that had all amassed on the bedside table over time.

A few minutes later, with the tray not being able to take any more, she carefully paced out of the room, shutting the door behind her with a furry pink slippered foot.

"Cheers, you fucking old slag," responded Whiff.

I had changed my views on Whiff's off-colour comments to his mum since I had first heard them, as shocking as they were, they were hilarious when you thought about it. Whiff's mum was probably one of the nicest people you could ever care to meet,

219

loving, open-minded, caring, she thought the world of him, his reaction to her was so over the top, so ridiculous that you'd either laugh or cry. I decided to laugh and now, right in front of me, Custer was crying with laughter, tears running down his cheeks.

"Yeah, you fucking old slag," said Custer, raising his voice.

Yeah, it is funny, I thought, but it's not for you to say, is it? She's Whiff's mum, shame you didn't say that to the unholy trinity, at the back of Ware college, but you were too busy colouring your boxer shorts brown, sprinting away to safety, weren't you?

It was a long ten minutes later when Custer said, "I've got to go now." I almost stood up and cheered.

"I better go, I'm meeting the lads down the Punch house," he told us.

I peeped my eyes open, saw he was wearing his bondage trousers, with his Discharge t-shirt, and I wondered if he was going to go home and get changed first.

"I'll call some of the London lot from mine on the way down, make sure they're coming," he said, clearing it up for me.

Whiff said, "OK, see ya mate and bring a few with you."

"I will mate I will, I just hope there's enough room for us all," said Custer, grinning inanely.

"Nice one, David," said Whiff happily, getting up to walk his mate to the door.

A few minutes later, Whiff came back in, "I don't know what's up with you Skin, he's alright, he is."

"Yeah, sorry man I'm just knackered, let's get some kip shall we."

I couldn't be bothered to go over all of that again; it was up to him.

Whiff nodded sleepily, kicked back on his bed and within a couple of minutes we both dozed off into a deep sleep, waking around five o'clock, when Judy came in, asking us if we wanted anything to eat, or drink, an offer that we both jumped at. A bit of grub consumed, we splashed some water on our faces, then strolled back down into the centre of Ware, meeting up Dave and Andy at Founder's Hall around six o'clock and despite all of our sleep deprivation we were all in good spirits and ready to play.

Andy pushed through the light brown outer doors, entering into the porch area, the rest of us following close behind, where we heard a hubbub of voices, coming from the main hall. Dave looked at me quizzically, I shrugged my shoulders, pushed down onto the large metal bar of the inner door, which flew open to reveal the hall was full of people. Not our people, either.

A huge crowd of families were seated in circles around several circular tables, chatting, laughing, drinking mugs of tea or coffee and picking at a large array of sandwiches, in front of them. In amongst the sandwiches, open Tupperware boxes full of cakes, were being feasting on by ravenous children whilst they avidly drew pictures or studied school exercise books. One group of youngsters ran wild up and down a large walkway, that ran in between the tables squealing, shouting and laughing, much to their parent's behest.

Dave, Andy, Whiff and me strolled down the walkway, dodging shrieking kids to the opposite end of the hall, put our gear down and returned for another load. On the second load, one of the out of control kids careered headfirst into Dave's bass drum case, bouncing off it like a fledgling on a window, onto the floor and immediately started blubbing.

A young Dad swooped in, picked up the sobbing infant in his comforting arms, scrutinizing Dave, who put his hand to say he was sorry.

I cracked a small smile, "Nice one Dave, that's a good start, you just pole-axed a little kid."

"Yeah, be careful Dave, he could have been one of Andy's mates," said a smirking Whiff.

Andy laughed, fixing Whiff with a lopsided grin, "Oi he's not just a friend, he's my best friend I was hoping to play Lego with him later."

"Bloody hell mate, you can't even walk into a hall without some little kid throwing himself at your drum kit," said Dave in full on Alan mode.

Once we had set up, we sat back watching, waiting, watching and wondering when all these people were going to leave, so we could play a couple of tracks to warm up, maybe make some adjustments to our limited sound; no one was moving though. I noticed there was a funny smell in the air, a smell of cat's piss, so I exaggeratedly lifted my head sniffing at the air, like a meerkat.

"Yeah, what is that fucking stink? It smells like my nan's old people's home," Whiff groaned.

"I think it's broccoli," said Dave. "It stinks, doesn't it?

Andy inhaled deeply, "It does, it's all the sulphur in it, I like broccoli it's good for you," he said.

Whiff rolled his eyes, "Yeah, you would."

Andy cackled. "Oh Paul, eat your greens, and you'll grow up a big strong boy," He Judy-ed.

I snorted, "Don't worry about that, he had some 'Greens' last night, didn't you Whiff?"

Whiff Punched his fist into the air, "Sensimelia."

Whiff and me both cracked up laughing, Andy and Dave, just looked at each other blankly.

An hour went by and none of the people who said they were coming, had shown up and worse still none of the people who were supposed to be going, were showing any signs of leaving either. I was beginning to feel bored, frustrated and not just a little bit angry, so I plugged my guitar into my amp, jacked the volume right up, hit a huge Bar E chord, making the stage tremble, in the vain hope that they would take the hint and start packing up. I was wrong, as the glorious E faded away out of the din of conversation, someone shouted.

"What a load of rubbish!"

A few people laughed and then the whole hall burst into song,

What a load of rubbish, what a load of rubbish, what a load of rubbish!
What a load of rubbish, what a load of rubbish, what a load of rubbish!

Andy began conducting them, and they booed back at him.

"What the fucking hell's going on, Andy? It's like the place is double-booked or something."

"I don't know, but I'm going to go and find out, this really is a load of rubbish," Andy said tersely, jumping down off the stage.

I said to Dave and Whiff, "Where the fucking hell is everyone? This is a fucking disaster."

"It's a joke," Dave agreed.

What a load of rubbish, what a load of rubbish, what a load of rubbish!
What a load of rubbish, what a load of rubbish, what a load of rubbish!

"Oh, hold on," said Whiff, looking expectantly at the opening double doors.

David the cowardly Custer Cowley walked in on his own, waving glibly at us.

Whiff shouted over to him, "I thought you were coming with your mates?"

"Oh, yeah they couldn't make it, sorry Whiff, if it was tomorrow everyone would be here," he lied pathetically.

Surprise, surprise, what a wanker, I thought.

What a load of rubbish, what a load of rubbish, what a load of rubbish!
What a load of rubbish, what a load of rubbish, what a load of rubbish!

A few minutes later, the door bounced open again, we looked up in hope, and a cluster of young mums came in behind push chairs, followed moments later by, oh, thank fuck for that, Phil, Jo Williams, Taddy, Danny, Hayley, Mucus holding hands with Lucy Flat Chesterman, Craig, Mark 'Bondy' Bond, Basher, his sister Carol, Gary, Simon, Matt, a couple of the Onslaught lads, Glyn, Lee, Ronnie, Gobber, and last, but not least from my point of view, Mark Palmer with Cerys, which not only put an end to the singing, it made us all feel a whole lot better. Andy's mates showed up a bit later too, and I thought, that's fine, OK it's time for us to go on now, whoever these people are, or whatever their game is, hopefully they will go now.

Dave grabbed Andy's mic and began to make a political speech pretending the mic was broken and kept cutting out, he was brilliant at it, we were all falling about laughing

What a load of rubbish, what a load of rubbish, what a load of rubbish, what a load of rubbish, what a load of rubbish, what a load of rubbish!

Dave stopped his speech and glanced at me, "Oh dear, oh dear, oh dear, tough crowd."

225

Andy came pounding back, got up onto the stage, Dave handed him his mic, "I wish you luck mate, tough crowd, it's a tough crowd," Dave said slapping his forehead, melodramatically.

"Who are they, Andy, and when are they going to fuck off?" I asked, staring at the wankers.

Andy ran his hand through his spikes, clearly agitated, "It's a community group called The Late, Late Breakfast Club, for people who are too busy in the morning."

"Ooh, snappy name," Whiff said.

I shot him a look, "OK, so when are they going to fuck off?"

"I don't think they are Skinner; they were booked until seven, but so many people have come that they're going to extend it till nine now," he said bitterly, grinding his teeth.

"Nah, fuck that, I'm not sitting here for another hour, go and announce us!" I demanded.

What a load of rubbish, what a load of rubbish, what a load of rubbish!
What a load of rubbish, what a load of rubbish, what a load of rubbish!

Andy hesitated, I pressed, "Come on Andy, I'm not listening to these cunts any more."

"OK then," he said, taking a deep breath.

"Nor am I," said Whiff, flicking the switch on his amp.

"Yeah, let's do it," said Dave, unleashing a roll on his snare.

What a load of rubbish, what a load of rubbish, what a load of
rubbish!
What a load of rubbish, what a load of rubbish, what a load of
rubbish!

I nodded to my mates, always ready to back each other up, "Yeah,
let's blow Founder's Hall away."

"What a load of rubbish, what a load of rubbish, what a load of
rubbish, what a load of rubbish" we sang back at them, with Andy
conducting us this time.

Andy drew the mic up and smirked, "OK, good evening, we are
Virus V1, and we are a punk band. I repeat, we are a punk band!"

An expectant silence came over the hall, as the amused singers
waited for our next move.

A couple of little kids ran down the middle aisle screaming, giggling,
breaking the silence and the singers cheered their offspring,
delighting in another humiliation of the scruffy punks on up on stage
who thought they were better than The Late, Late, Breakfast Club.

"I've had enough of this bullshit," I said, "We'll skip 'Everybody's
Boy', go straight to 'Christ Fuckers', and when I say Christ Fuckers,
Andy, I mean Christ fuckers. Not C.F."

Dave threw his head back, cackling insanely, clicking his sticks
together, "Yeah, nice one, Skin, 'Christ Fuckers'."

227

What a load of rubbish, what a load of rubbish, what a load of rubbish, what a load of rubbish, what a load of rubbish, what a load of rubbish… started up again.

Andy grinned mercilessly, "Yeeahh, OK." Andy drew the mic back up again, "OK… So yeah… Good evening! Before we start, I'd just like to say, since you're not our usual type of audience, we've changed our set especially for you… this is our first number it's called… 'CHRIST FUCKERS'!"

Whiff, chest puffed out, strutted to the front of the stage, "You hear that? It's called CHRIST FUCKERS, CHRIST FUCKERS, CHRIST FUCKERS, CHRIST FUCKERS…" making sure they heard… they heard alright.

At once, the singing stopped and apart from the hum from our amps, the hall was completely silent, you could have heard half a pin drop. A couple of little kids stood frozen, open-mouthed gawking up at us from the dividing walkway, behind them, it was exactly the same, Dads, Mums and Grandparents were gaping, horrified, at what they had heard, wondering, what was coming next. I observed them with a cold clear eye, fuck them, I thought, what goes around comes around, now I knew what the phrase, 'deafening sound of silence' means.

Dave cut through that silence, hitting the intro and Andy started the chant, "Symbol of religion a man in pain, Jesus died well what a shame, so that you might be forgiven, sin is what you live in… well you can fuck your own Christ…"

I heard some shouting, looked up from my fret board to see some of the younger Dads standing up, pointing, shouting furiously, putting their fists up, their wives at their side holding them back, trying to calm them down, stop them from murdering the punk rockers.

"Fuck off!" I mouthed to them, revelling in the payback.

A couple of old war veterans in blue blazers, black berets, medals dangling at their chest, waved their walking sticks at us, with faces steadfast, thunderous, unblinking in the presence of the enemy, wobbling on their world-weary legs. Not singing now are you fucking old bastards, I thought.

"You say we live in sin; I say I owe fuck all to your king," Andy bellowed, and they wilted like turds in bleach.

A whole floor seemed to get up and walk as people gave up, deciding on a tactical retreat, tables were cleared, bags hurriedly packed, crying kids were grabbed by their arms and strapped into pushchairs, before they could hear any more of this filth.

In the time it took us to play 'Christ Fuckers', The Late, Late Breakfast Club, 'for people who are too busy in the morning', had cleared out of the hall, and as 'Christ Fuckers' came to its sweet end, the door shut on the arse of the last of them, sending us into fits of laughter.

One of the double doors crashed inwards, a woman of about forty years old appeared, "I think your music, if you can call it that, is disgusting," she shrieked, hysterically.

Whiff stepped forward, "I'm sorry,"

She fell silent, studying him for a moment, "Yes, and so you should be."

"I'm sorry," repeated Whiff, a small grin playing at the corner of his lips.

"Yes, yes, OK," she said, wondering what was wrong with this cretinous punk rocker.

"Nah, I mean, I'm sorry I said I was sorry," Whiff interjected.

"What? I don't understand, what are you talking about?"

"I'm sorry I said I was sorry, because I'm not sorry, none of us are," Whiff grinned.

"Oh, I see. Yes, very funny, well I'll make sure you never play at the Founder's Hall again."

I snorted. "Oh no, we're so upset," I mewled sarcastically,

"You can stick Flounder's Hall up your flabby arse, you stupid old cow."

"What did you say?"

"I said. Stick. It. Up. Your. Flabby. Arse."

She looked like she was going to burst into tears. "I think it's disgusting, you're disgusting," she said, as her parting shot, and slammed the door so hard the hall shook.

Dave stood up from behind his drum kit, grinning, "Not a Virus V1 fan, then?"

"Nah, definitely not, mate, she didn't give us a chance though, did she? She only stayed for one track," I stated factually.

In the moment or so it took us to calm down, I looked at our audience of about twenty and thought, if they were good enough to make the effort to come and see us, then we should make the effort too; even Custer deserves a few tracks, there was some trouble and he didn't leg it this time.

"Shall we play!?" I asked.

"Definitely!" Dave said picking up his sticks.

"Yeah, come on, it'll be like a practice, a practice in front of our mates," Whiff smiled.

Andy nodded; a big smile erupting onto his face, he drew up the mic, "Halloo, good evening, as you probably know by now, we are Virus V1. I'd like to dedicate our whole set to The Late, Late Breakfast Club, particularly the stupid old bag with the wobbly bum who just walked out, this one's called, 'Everybody's Bum'."

Virus V1 launched into the set, playing our full twelve tracks with all the energy and anger that we usually did, and as our final track V1 Bomb came to its end, we thought it was all worth it, as we received a generous round of applause from our friends, the people who really mattered. Andy, Whiff, Dave clapped them back, while I pulled the curtains closed from the wings, leaving a gaping hole at the end. I peeped through the gap and saw Cerys was standing alone outside the toilet at the front of the hall, my mind said, go, go, go, so I quickly zipped up my guitar safely into its case, hopped down off the stage and casually wandered over to see how she was.

"Aaah… Don't tell me… Mark's left as well, has he?" I asked, a smile developing on my face.

"Oh no, he's in the toilet… he's probably doing his hair again," she said, raising her eyebrows expansively.

"Oh what, he's not that bad, is he?"

"Yeah, it's been…" she checked her watch.

"Hmmm, it's been about five minutes now."

"You sure he hasn't jumped out the window?"

"If he has, that's it for us," she said playfully.

"Oh well, at least something good will have come out of tonight," I ventured.

"It wasn't that bad; it was just a bad audience; I don't know what they were expecting," She said, ignoring my venture.

I let out a deep sigh, shaking my head, "Nah that was shit, it's not going to get me out of the village, is it?"

"It's only your third gig, I really enjoyed it. I don't think The Late, Late, Breakfast Club did though," she said, her face opening into a smile. "I've never seen people move so quickly," she added, the smile blossoming into a sweet laugh.

"It was an exodus, wasn't it, I wonder if they'll let us play here again?" I said, smiling innocently.

"Hmm… No, probably not," she said, falling about laughing.

Mark came out of the toilet, a couple of minutes later, his hair perfectly spiked up. Cerys and me exchanged a glance.

Mark looked at us questioningly. "Oh, alright Skinner, good gig, I enjoyed it." he said passing a hand through his hair.

"Hi Mark, cheers for coming man."

"Loved every minute of it mate, especially 'Christ Fuckers' great song, good reaction too," he said, laughing.

"Cheers, Mark, I'll tell you what, why don't you two come along to our next rehearsal?"

Cerys said, "Yeah, I'd like that, OK." Nodding her head over excitedly.

"OK cool, nice one, maybe we can get a carry-out or something, have a couple of drinks down there, you up for that Mark?" I suggested.

"Yeah, yeah, yeah maybe, I don't know, we'll have to see what we're up to won't we Cerys?" Mark said, putting a protective arm around his girlfriend.

"OK, up to you mate, I might see you then yeah? Come down, it'll be a laugh, anyway, look I'd better go help Dave with his drums, it's hard work this punk rock life you know."

233

Chapter 12

It's Fucking Whisky Time

It was around this time that Andy produced his first test tape, I was pleased to see that he had followed the original format by writing the full twelve tracks, so there was an album feel to it. In amongst some decent tracks, a couple of tape fillers, a real gem of a track, 'Horrors of Belsen' stood out. It was a slow grinding number with a nasty key change between verse and chorus, lyrically, the subject matter was something very close to our hearts. I told him we should have it in our set, and he was made up about it, telling me confidently that it was the best track he had written, so far anyway. 'So far', I thought, wow, it's his first test tape, and he's written a track like this, good, we need more tracks like this for Virus V1.

A few days of playing 'Horrors of Belsen' on my mum's dilapidated old cassette player told me that it was a missed opportunity, it was such a great track, but coming in at just under one minute eight seconds, it finished way too soon, for me. 'Horrors of Belsen' needed something else, an intro, a middle eight or maybe even a bridge, a new verse, anything, something to double the length of it; the guitar riffs were so good, so mesmerising that they would carry the track, long after one minute eight seconds. Virus V1 had plenty of 'one-minute wonders', they were all fast though, our slower tracks usually came in around two and half minutes, the idea being that you could immerse yourself in them, pay more attention to the lyrics, rather than chucking yourself around to them like on the fast ones.

I broached the subject with Andy, and I was disappointed. He reckoned he didn't want to extend it, and if people wanted to hear the riffs more, then they would have to play the track over again, which seemed like a missed opportunity to me, so I persevered. In

234

the end, we agreed that we would work on the track with the other two, as a band, sticking to his original track. If Dave or Whiff came up with anything that he liked, then we would put it in, which made perfect sense to me. After all, it was his track, and that was the whole point of having another songwriter in the band, to make our tracks more varied. Whiff had shown some interest in writing too, which I thought could be different, with his love of American hardcore thrash, as for Dave he was never interested, he just wanted to smash the shit out of his drum kit.

I hastily put together a new test tape including some of Andy's tracks on it for Whiff and Dave to listen to, and they both agreed that we should bring 'Horrors of Belsen' into our set. Virus V1 tracks 'Monarchy' and 'Curfew' were written around the time of inception of the band, they sounded primitive compared to some of the newer tracks I had waiting to go in my song folder, so I thought it was time to drop them and freshen the set-up with something else.

Dave and Whiff had mentioned another track on the new test tape called 'Auschwitz 84'. It was a fast, furious audio assault and although the titles were similar, I didn't think we'd be repeating our message, as even though the subject was the same, the content was very different. Horrors of Belsen was about remembrance, respect, a warning from history about the evils of totalitarian states, graphic in its concentration camp descriptions to smash the message home, whereas Auschwitz 84 was a homage to George Orwell's book 1984, but instead of the dystopian world he had predicted, I painted a corrosive picture of a world where the bigotry and blind hatred caused by the rise of nationalism through Thatcherism and the march of the NF skinhead movement, led to a world where the cattle trucks would roll again.

Dave and me went through both of them on our unofficial Friday
night practice, I asked Dave to use Rudimentary Peni's tracks 'The
Gardener' for 'Horrors of Belsen' and 'Bloody Jellies' for 'Auschwitz
84' as guidance for the beats. Dave being an expert in Rudimentary
Peni drum beats and a big fan of Jon Greville knocked them out
straight away. By the time we went through them the third time, he
started changing them, putting in his own touches, making them his
own. 'Horrors of Belsen' still wasn't reaching its full potential as far
as I concerned and pretty soon Dave saw it too, it was definitely
going to need something else. A few ideas later, we were all out of
ideas, it was still lacking something, so with Dave off to see Steph
and me off for my usual Friday night visit to snakebite land, we left it
for the next morning, maybe the four of us would be able to work
something out then.

On Saturday morning, Andy walked into the pavilion with a broad
smile on his face, telling us that he had got us a gig at The Triad
Club in Bishop's Stortford, supporting a local punk band called The
Filthy Habitz. He reckoned that this time there would be a decent
crowd in, as The Filthy Habits were local lads, had a good punk fan
base in and around Stortford, around Harlow too, which sounded
good. A simple gig playing in front of punks like us, thank fuck I
thought.

"Oh, well done Andy, nice one!" I said, nodding,

"It's not going to be another, The Late, Late breakfast club for
wankers too lazy to get out of bed in the morning, is it?" I joked.

"No, this one should be better… it can't be any worse anyway, can
it?" Asked Andy, raising his thick eyebrows up and down like
Groucho Marx.

Whiff walked in, carrying his boom box under his arm. Yes, I thought, tapping my pocket, making sure that I had brought the punk covers test tape that I had been working on with me. I felt the bulge, suppressed a laugh, it was a surprise for everyone, because in amongst the Discharge, GBH and Crass tracks, there was a version of The Exploited's track 'Exploited Barmy Army', only I had changed it to 'Whiffy Barmy Army'.

Whiff held the bulky grey boom box above his head announcing, "I've found an album by an Italian death metal band called Bulldozer, listen to this, it's our new anthem Skin."

Whiff banged the volume right up and Bulldozer's singer screamed, "It's fucking whisky time!", leading into a massive explosion of guitars, and then all hell broke loose. He cracked up laughing, banging his head along with the mayhem, I wasn't sure about death metal, or metal in general, I liked this though. It was classic, definitely something we could relate to, as over the last week, we too had discovered the delights of whisky on one of our pub crawls in Ware.

Andy laughed, "Bloody hell, I thought we were a racket."

"It's fucking whisky time!" Screamed Whiff in such a high pitch that it didn't seem possible for someone of his gargantuan size to have made that noise.

Dave creased up, "Jesus, do it again, do it again!"

Whiff laughed, lifted his head up, "Weeeeeeeeeeeeeeee!"

"I'm gonna make you squeal like a pig. Squeal piggy, Squeal piggy," drawled Dave in an American southern state's accent, sounding like a mountain man from the film Deliverance.

"Weeeeeeeeeeeeeeeeee," responded Whiff.

"Oh what, that hurt my ears, have your bollocks actually dropped Whiff?" I asked.

Dave said, "That's a little bit harsh, isn't it?"

"Harsh realities of life, my friend," I parroted back.

"It's not fucking whisky time; it's fucking new track time," Andy said excitedly, picking up his mic.

Dave nodded and flipped a roll on his snare, I turned my guitar, while Whiff carried on head banging.

"Come mate, let's make a start on Horrors," I said.

"OK," said Whiff, pushing the off button on his boom box, ending fucking whisky time, for now.

Whiff picked up his bass, Dave hit his beat, and tentatively we began running through it, it was a simple track, verse, chorus, verse, chorus and we progressed quickly, the only trouble was every time the four elements of the track, vocals, guitar, bass and drums began to entwine, feel hypnotic, taking you somewhere else, it ended.

"It still needs something else Andy," I suggested, hopefully, "How about an intro?"

Andy nodded. "Yeah, OK, maybe, give it a go, it needs something different on the bass too," he looked to Whiff, Whiff nodded back.

On the sixth run through, I slashed a couple of chords at the start, holding them down as an intro and as they faded into Dave's rhythm, from somewhere I don't know where, Whiff came up with an incredible bass line. It was ghostly, grinding, sat perfectly between Andy's gliding guitar riffs and the thump of Dave's bass drum. Yes, I thought, that is a classic, I wondered whether he should play that all the way through. It was certainly good enough, and as the track ended not so soon this time.

Andy said, "Whiff that's brilliant, keep playing all the way through on the verses."

I nodded at Andy, "Good idea, mate."

A couple more run throughs and 'Horrors' was shaping up nicely, so happy with our progress, we turned our attention to the more familiar thrash territory of Auschwitz '84. A new track like Auschwitz '84 should be easy after 'Horrors', I thought, as it had been written, in the same model as our other fast tracks 'Protest' and 'No more Genocide'. It turned out to be anything but, because of that very reason. It had to be different, we couldn't just play twelve different versions of the same track live, so we speeded it up a lot, that helped, and we added an intro, which also helped, it still wasn't there though, it needed something else to distinguish it from our other thrashers. I asked Andy if he could come up with something different, make the track unique, stand out amongst the others, and he said he had an idea. So he sat back and let us run through it a few times to get the music right, then he added a series of pain ridden guttural screams after each chorus. It was horrifying, it was chilling, it was brilliant, it was something we hadn't done before, and we were now well on the way to adding two new tracks to the set.

In the last half an hour of our practice we set about polishing both tracks up, and played them repeatedly until the first group of football players walked into the pavilion, looking around wondering what the racket was, as usual. Once we had packed away our gear safely into the back of Dave's van, we sat outside on a bench underneath the pavilion window, taking in the warm early afternoon sunshine. Whiff and me broke out the roll ups, whilst Andy and Dave talked about sport.

I took a huge lung full, "I'm not sure about playing the new ones live yet, shall we see how we feel after the next practice?"

Andy, Dave and Whiff nodded in agreement, so we arranged our next practice for Friday, the night before the gig, so we could go through them and see if we could do them justice live.

I felt the tape in my pocket. It was time.

"Oh yeah, I've got a surprise for you lot, give us the boom box Whiff."

Whiff grinned, obligingly handing it over to me. I pulled the tape from the inside pocket of my leather jacket, stuck it in, pressed play and stood back grinning. I watched everyone's faces; it was just as I expected. It's not a bad version of 'Exploited Barmy Army' they said, the vocals started spelling out his name, they looked puzzled, and then when the chorus came in, they all collapsed into fits of laughter, chanting along,

"Whiffy Barmy Army, Whiffy Barmy Army, Whiffy Barmy Army, don't mess!" Pumping their fists in the air.

A couple of football players came out of the pavilion with their strips on, telling Dave that he had better get a move on, so he left us to get ready for his afternoon's football match, while the rest of us walked down to The Anchor chanting Whiff's theme tune, and when we got there, it was fucking whisky time for Whiff and me, it couldn't have been anything else.

*

On the Friday night before the Bishop Stortford gig, we met at Dave's house early, all of us keen to get down to the pavilion, set up and play. I had heard a lot of good things about The Triad club, in the intervening week, it was not only a decent venue, but it was a decent venue for local punk bands. Chron Gen, with support from Chaos Crew, had played there only a few weeks before, The Triad had been packed out, this could be our next step, I thought.

Once we had got the gear down to the pavilion in the yellow AD marina, we began to set up in earnest. It was the practice before the gig, the rallying call, a time of unity, everyone was well up for it, excited about the weekend that lay in front of us.

Dave slid his mounted toms into holding at the front of the bass drum, "Oh yeah, you know Reg Cooper, the grounds man?" He asked, screwing them in tight.

"What's he been moaning about now?" I asked.

"No, it's nothing like that, he told my old man that he likes our music, he reckons he listens to us as he does the pitches on Saturday morning."

Andy, eyes focused on putting another bit of tape on his brand-new mic, "What? Is he a punk rocker then?"

"I doubt it, he's an old bloke, he must be fifty," I scoffed.

Dave began screwing them securely into place, "I can't imagine him pacing up and down with the line marker shouting, 'Fuck the state, we don't need it'."

I watched the needle on my tuner bounce frustratingly away from A, once again. "How about Fuck the rake?" I ventured.

Whiff snorted, "Reg Cooper is our number one fan, yeahhhhh come on Reginald."

"Our only fan, more like," said Andy.

"Nah my mum likes us, well she did, she's gone off us though." I added, "I tell you; nothing surprises me in this village anymore, I saw Hilary on the way down this morning, he looked like he was talking to a tree in his garden."

Dave, Whiff and Andy stopped what they were doing and creased up laughing.

"Sure, you did Skin, tell us about it," said Dave, shaking his head, not believing a word of it, hoping it was true.

"Seriously, when I got close, he saw me and watched me go past, not moving his head at all, it was just his eyes moving, right to left, all the way round."

Once again, the three of them cracked up laughing.

"It was that weirdo Baker, walking through my Garden of Eden," Dave Hilary-ed.

"His Garden of Eden? Can you imagine Tamara in the Garden of Eden with her fig leaf?" I asked.

"No Skin, I can't, I really don't want to," said Dave, pulling a horrified face.

Whiff snorted, "She'd need more than a fig leaf, she's massive."

"I bet she'd be happier in the Garden of Edam," I ventured.

Whiff cackled, scratched his dark stubbly chin, "I don't know about you lot, but I fancy a drink, let's get some whisky." He screamed in falsetto, "It's fucking whisky time!"

Dave and Andy weren't interested, I was, though, very interested, it was the express route.

I checked to see if I still had that crumpled fiver in my pocket, I did, "Yeah OK, let's do it."

Whiff threw his hands in the air. "It's fucking whisky time," he squealed, both of us cackling madly.

"The Anchor?" I suggested.

"That'll do nicely."

Whiff and me left the pavilion to the sounds of Andy playing 'Horrors' on my guitar. We strode around the back, across the open fields to the river rib, passing the familiar fishing sites of the third dam, the pipe and the fast waters, where my mum and me caught trout when I was a little kid, putting them back in of course, we never wanted to eat them. Once we had passed the fast waters, we ambled up a steep slope at the side of the bridge, stopping at a small ledge that ran around a deep ravine to the side of it. I pointed to the foot wide pathway, telling him to be careful, as I had seen an old mate of mine, Kev 'King of the Blockheads' Green, fall into it when me and Dave were back at the Junior Mental Institution.

Kev, Dave, Trotsky and me had been side stepping around the ledge, Kev bringing up the rear, when I heard a loud wail, a crumpling of twigs, and I had spun around to find Kev had vanished. A moment later, a pathetic, mewling sound resonated from the depths of the ravine, then a hand reached up out of the stinging nettles below, begging for help. Dave and Trotsky carefully descended into the ravine, gaining purchase on the hapless Kev, they pushed him up the bank, while I took his hands, pulling him back up onto the ledge. Once we had got back up to the top, he brightened up, in fact he was fine, only a bit shaken up by his fall, so Dave went into full piss taking mode. Dave wandered around the now grinning Kev, hand on chin like he was Doctor Heinz Wolff, looking into a particularly puzzling case.

"Hmm yes, hmm yes, very interesting, hmm yes, hmm yes, I think I see ziz one... I'm not one hundred percent zertain, but I would zay he's chipped a corner, yes, yes, he has chipped a corner of his blockhead, he's chipped a corner," he diagnosed.

Whiff standing next to me now, I stared down gaping into it, and I was surprised Kev hadn't broken his fucking neck; it was so deep. I casually walked around the ledge, looked back, watching with some amusement as Whiff, nervously, baby stepped his way across. I wondered what would happen if I shouted something right now. It was irresistible.

"BLOODY HELL HAMMERSMITH, COME ON, YOU WON'T GET IN THE ARMY LIKE THAT MOOOOOOOOOOOOVVVVVVVVVVE!" I Alan- ed at maximum volume.

Whiff jolted forward, arms spinning, pin wheeling, trying to keep balance, "Ahh, fucking hell, Skin don't do that."

I smirked, "You're such a townie, Whiff."

Whiff grinned back at me, nodding, "Yeah, and with good reason too. I like pavements, you can't actually fall off them and die."

Once we had successfully traversed Block Chip Falls, we carried on over the bridge, taking in the Thundridge illuminations as we went, even in the twilight, the last of them still shone brightly, pulsating out from the depths, like E.T. phoning home. Whiff and me zoned out on them for a while, then crossed the bridge and went into The Anchor to begin the process of fucking whisky time.

Whiff ordered us a half bottle of Bell's whisky.

"Skin, it doesn't have the best taste, but it's cheap and does the job," he told me.

Cheap and does the job! I liked the sound of that, so I handed over my crumpled fiver, took the bottle, and we started back.

Whiff and me went back around Block Chip Falls, safe now, I unscrewed the bottle and took a swig. It tasted fine to me, so I necked about a quarter of it in three long drafts. Immediately, the spirit warmed and cleansed me as it spread its way through my body, radiating through my veins like central heating. I thought, oh yeah, I like this, let's have some more.

A Whiff attached hand reached out and grabbed it, "Whoa, take it easy, Skin, let's have some."

Whiff took a decent couple of glugs for himself, then wiping the dark brown fluid from his chin he handed it back, so in the heat of the moment, enjoying the heat inside me, I drained the bottle in one go, casually chucking it over my shoulder, into the River Rib.

H.M.S. Bell's Scotch whisky bottle, bobbed off down the river as the current caught it, it was then snatched at by low stinging nettles at the water's edge, where it flipped, spun, dipped, finally releasing itself, only to run into a fallen branch, where it slowly edged its way along the sturdy brown wood until the current caught it once more, and it headed out into open water.

"Oi, oi, are you alright, Skin?" Whiff nudged me.

"Yeah, I think show," I returned.

He laughed, "I was talking to you mate, you were miles away."

I looked down at my feet, they seemed to be miles way too, like I was high up on stilts. Oh what, look at my feet why are they so far beneath me, left, right, left, right, left, right, left, right, moving all on their very own, I thought, cracking up laughing.

I wasn't doing anything, they just stepped, I snorted, cackled some more, "Whey… Whiffy Barmy Army, Whiffy Barmy Army. You alright mate?"

Whiff grinned, "I reckon you've just drunk fourteen measures of whisky, you nutter."

"I'm in the Scottish Highlands now mate, och I der fuckin noo," I said, stumbling forward as one of my auto-feet failed to make the correct contact with the earth.

Whiff burst out laughing, putting a hand out.

"Whoa," I said from my high perch. "You know what, it really is fucking whisky time," said I, feebly punching at the air.

"It might be for you mate, but it's not for me, I only had a couple of sips."

"I think I might have over done it, mate," I conceded.

Whiff nodded in agreement, "Fucking, have you."

I belched horribly, felt sick rising up in my stomach, then as the pavilion came into view, I saw my salvation, thinking it's not a problem now, because my other two best mates are in there, and not only that, we're in a band, and we're going to have the best practice we've ever had.

I stumbled in through the pavilion door using the frame for balance, and I saw Dave, "Oh, there he is, Dave! You alright mate?"

Dave peered at me curiously from over his drum kit, laughed, looked at Whiff for an explanation, who grinned and shrugged his shoulders back at him. Andy was here too, he's a fucking brilliant singer he is, I thought. I grabbed his hand, pumping it vigorously up and down.

"Andy, Andy!" I enthralled, "Are you alright?"

All of my mates were laughing their heads off, I thought I must've said something funny, so I burst out laughing too, joining in with them,

"Come on, let's practice, let's do V1 bomb, I fucking love that track, it's brilliant, V...1... bomb!" I almost sang.

I sat down heavily, grabbed my guitar, and fumbled the plectrum from in-between the strings at the top neck. Ready, I looked at the others expectantly.

Dave looked over at Whiff again, said something, Whiff shook his head.

"Skin, shall we just do the set?" Whiff asked.

"Yeah, yeah, yeah, let's do the set, it's fucking brilliant," I agreed with my best mate.

Dave nodded and hit the intro to 'Everybody's Boy'. We were off, I was concentrating as hard as I could, thinking, this is the best I've ever played, Dave stopped, and we came to a grinding halt.

"What's up, Dave?" I asked, surprised.

Dave sighed, "Bloody hell, how much has he had?"

"A lot," said Whiff.

"A lot!" I echoed, smiling, liking the sound of a lot.

"He must have done three quarters of the bottle, maybe more, I'm surprised he hasn't fucking passed out," said Whiff.

Dave grinned, shook his head slowly, "Fucking hell, Skin!"

"What? I can still fucking play you know, come on, let's do it. I'll be fine once we get going, I just need to warm up a bit," I said huffily.

Dave sighed. "OK, Skin, what do you want to play?" He said indulgently.

I belched, tasting whisky, cheese on toast, a chow mein pot noodle and many Roll Up's.

"Ah yeah let's do Whiffy Barmy Army, no, no, no, Christ Fuckers, that track is fucking brilliant, in fact, it's fuckers brilliant," I laughed at my own non joke.

I felt my stomach cramp up hideously and released it with a huge, sickly belch.

"Euuuugh, Jesus, are you alright Skin, you're not going to throw up, are you?"

I leant forward cradling my rapidly cramping stomach, my head flew forwards with the momentum, and the floor bounced up hazardously pitching left, right in front of my disbelieving eyes. So I shut them in a vain attempt to block it all out, but the rolling was inside my head too.

Virus V1 were going to play tonight, it was the last practice before the gig, the rallying call, and we're going to play 'Christ Fuckers' now, so I gave the now blurred Dave a sideways thumbs up. Dave hit the intro; Andy started the chant. I sat bolt upright in my chair and proudly hit the first chord, coming in on time, I nodded along, this is brilliant I thought, then slowly, steadily, like a sandcastle being eroded by the sea, I slumped further and further forward over my guitar and by the middle of the track, my head was closer to the floor than my guitar was. I righted myself, looked over at my mates, thinking about all the things we've done, all the things we've been through, and I felt a surge of comradery, then the door edged open.

A smiling Cerys walked into the pavilion on her own. I thought brilliant no Mark, so I stopped playing, jumped up, leant my guitar against a table and ran over to see my old girlfriend.

"Whey… Cerys, what are you doing here?" I asked.

BAAAAAAM KERAAAAANG… My guitar crashed to the floor.

SCCCCCCCRRRRRREEEEEEEEEEEEEEE… Feedback ripped our ears.

Andy quickly ran over, picked it up and turned the pick-ups off, silencing it.

"What the fuck, yeah, I yeah, my guitar, cheers Andy… What are you doing down here?" I asked, totally lost now.

Cerys gave me a peculiar look, "You invited me down, don't you remember?"

I couldn't. I nodded gormlessly.

"What's up with him?" She asked Dave.

"Ask him," Dave said, pointing an accusing finger at Whiff.

Whiff hauled a grimace onto his face, "Oh, he's a had a drink or two."

"Or three, or three hundred," Andy added, laughing hysterically.

"I'm fine, Cerys," I protested.

"Yeah, sure you are, Skinner," said Dave, fearing the worst.

Cerys scrutinized me closely, her eyes boring into my soul looking for answers, answers that were now floating around in a sea of whisky.

"I don't get it, he's not normally like that. What's he been drinking?"

"Whisky," said my mates in unison.

Oh, yeah whisky I thought, everything makes sense now, the floor stabilized, my eyes focused, I knew what I had to do.

I pulled down my trousers and boxers, pumped my arms in the air and shouted, "IT'S FUCKING WHISKY TIMEEEEEEEEEEEE!"

Cerys backed off, a worried look on her face, Dave pushed in between us, "Jeez… fucking hell Skin, don't do that."

Whiff put a placating hand on my shoulder. "Come on mate, pull them up, OK good, now come on let's go over here, come on."

Whiff and Andy took me by the arms, to the other side of the room, and we sat down.

"You alright, Skin let's have a roll up, you want a rolly, mate?" Whiff offered.

I nodded absently, watching Dave talking to my old girlfriend Cerys, I didn't know what they were saying, but they talked for what seemed like a very long a time. Cerys looked over at me swaying in my seat, hardly able to focus on Whiff's proffered roll up. I waved back in her general direction, gave her a drunken, lopsided grin, only for her face to cloud over, and she looked away, shaking her head in disgust. Dave pulled a smile, patted her on the shoulder and without a backwards glance, she marched out of the pavilion, slamming the door behind her. I puffed on my roll up, scratching at my aching head, furiously blinking my eyes, desperately trying to focus in on something, anything, everything was moving apart from me. I then became aware of the silence in the pavilion. I knew I had done something wrong; it was bad, very bad.

252

Dave broke the silence, "I thought you liked her, that was stupid mate, maybe whisky is not the best drink for you."

"Cheers for helping me out, you lot are alright, you are, good mates," I concluded.

Dave slapped his forehead, Andy and Whiff looked at each other.

"Fucking hell Skin," said Dave, stifling a laugh.

"You're my best mates, all of you," I announced, proudly.

Dave, Whiff and Andy all dissolved into fits of laughter, shaking their heads, slapping their foreheads for effect, I saw my mates were laughing, so I joined in too.

Chapter 13

Enter The Triad

I woke up the next morning - my bed felt warm, comfortable. The sun played gently around the edges of my curtains. I breathed in, stretched out and felt a series of aches in my shoulders. I rolled over and stretched again, pulling apart my limbs, easing the aches away. Inhaling deeply, I watched the cordial breeze rippling at my curtains, finding its way in. I tried to swallow, couldn't. My mouth was dry, dry and cotton like, I needed a drink. I needed a piss too. Inside my bed, it was so warm, though, both would have to wait. I rolled back over, studying the mellow beams of light around the curtains, thinking about the gig this evening.

A swarm of butterflies stretched their wings in my stomach, also waking up, nah it'll be fine, I thought, we've played in front of plenty of people before. A lot of different things have happened, but mostly it's been fun. I'm sure it'll be a good laugh whatever happens. I thought about the river, the pipe, the third dam, the oh yeah, Whiff laughing about Kevin Green's blockhead getting chipped at Block Chip Falls, the Thundridge illuminations, The Bells, The Bells whisky, the fucking whisky, the… Oh fucking hell, oh no… Cerys!!!

It all came flooding back, the floor pitching horribly, the sickening belches of nausea, a blurred vision of the pavilion, the looks of shock, pity, mirth of my mates, running at Cerys, flashing my dick at her, and finally, worst of all, the look on her face as she left the pavilion.

"That was stupid Skin."

Dave's words came back to me.

What I did that for? I don't know.

"That was stupid Skin."

I invited her down there to show her I wanted to do something with my life too.

"That was stupid Skin."

I thought I might be able to get her back.

"That was stupid Skin."

"That was stupid Skin."

"That was stupid Skin."

OK Dave, stop going on mate, I get it, 'bloody hell mate, have a heart' I internally Alan-ed. I knew the damage had been done, how could I limit that damage, well I couldn't, not lying here anyway, it was time to get up and think about this evening; think about the gig.

On with my bondage trousers, destroy shirt and least stinky socks, I plodded downstairs to find mum and the old man in the kitchen, having lunch. It was just another normal day in my house, my old man was ranting about some politician in the paper, or 'The Rag' as he called it, and my mum wasn't listening, she'd heard it all before.

My old man glanced up, rustling, in amongst the broad sheet, "Ah… It awakes. We thought you'd died."

I laughed and thought, I wish I had.

255

Mum smiled at her good-hearted, yet scruffy, rebellious son. "Good moaning," she said, in a bad French accent like the policeman off her favourite TV comedy 'Allo, Allo'. "And what are you doing today?"

"I thought I told you, we've got a gig tonight."

"No, no you didn't Mike, where is it?" She asked, enthusiastically.

"Bloody Michael Foot? Bloody Michael bloody Heal more like, what a big pile of dog turd," said the old man, from a different planet.

"It's over in Bishops Stortford," I said, ignoring him.

"Well done, that's great news!" Mum said, looking to the old man.

"What's this?" He said, slapping the rag down onto the table.

"Mike's band is playing tonight in Bishop's Stortford, Pudge," she said, using her pet name for him.

"Oh OK, well you be careful, money in the pop world is easy come, easy go."

I sighed, 'the pop world!!!' 'Money?', giving mum a patient smile, "Cheers for that Dad, if I see any, I will."

"And watch out for groupies."

I thought, yeah, now you're talking, I will lecherously.

My old man nodded sagely, picked up the rag, and got back to increasing his blood pressure.

"Oh, that's great news, Mike, it really is, you keep going, you'll get there one day!" My Mum smiled.

"One day… hopefully, mum," I said, loving the confidence she had in me.

Mum smiled, reached out and squeezed my hand.

"Thanks mum," I said, suddenly feeling a bit emotional.

I told her all about our gig while I ate my cornflakes and had a cup of tea, then after a quick wash in the bathroom, I left for Dave's feeling a lot better.

On the walk down to Dave's, I took in my surroundings, a bright yellow orb sun shone above, warming the green abundance around me, I couldn't look at it, I was jealous of its simple beauty, it seemed to mock me, as the dark remnants of last night pushed their way back to the surface.

"That was stupid Skin."

I know.

"That was stupid Skin."

Yes, I know.

"That was stupid Skin."

Oh, do fuck off.

In the kitchen at Dave's, it was its usual hive of activity, Jo and Hayley were standing by the fridge, wiping the sides down, chatting avidly, Ann was at the sink with Vicky, the youngest of the Williams girls, washing up the dinner plates.

Ann looked up and waved, her hands covered in suds, "Oh, hello Michael... I'm glad to see you've stopped that silly knocking on my door business, you know you're welcome here anytime!"

I smiled, "Thanks."

Dave walked out of the dining room, into the kitchen, joining us.

Hayley grinned at him, "Oh yes, hello Skinner. Did you enjoy your wee dram last night?"

I looked at Dave accusingly, and he smiled, shrugging his shoulders.

"What's this?" Asked Jo.

"Skinner's been a bad boy," Hayley taunted.

Jo sniggered, "What? Again?"

Hayley's face creased into a wicked smile, "Yes, he drank a bottle of whisky last night and flashed his willie at Cerys."

The whole room dissolved into a chorus of mirthful laughter.

Alan's head appeared around the side of the dining room door. "Bloody hell, Baker, what have you done now?" He asked, which had me splitting a smile too. "I thought you liked her."

"I do," I protested.

"You've got a funny way of showing it, bloody hell," said Alan, slapping his forehead.

Jo snorted, "It sounds like he showed her something, Dad."

"He certainly did," said Alan, cracking up.

"I doubt it was anything she hadn't seen before," Hayley shrieked with laughter.

Ann dried her hands, seeing I was beginning to feel uncomfortable. "Oh, don't listen to them, Michael. I'm sure everything will be fine; would you like a cup of tea?" She asked, coming to my rescue.

"Yeah, please, that would be brilliant, my mouth feels like I've been gargling with sand."

"Yes, I'm sure it does," she said, reaching for a cup.

Alan came into the kitchen, carrying his teacup with a big smile on his face, shaking his head slowly backwards and forwards. "Bloody...Old...Boy," he said, dumping his cup into the sink.

Dave repeated, "Bloody old boy." And we all creased up laughing.

Alan sighed loudly, "Come on then, Baker, what happened?"

I shook my head. "I don't remember much after I left the pub, sorry," I said honestly, hoping that would put an end to it.

Alan looked to Dave, it was too good to miss. Dave told them everything right from the start, everybody listening intently and as my tale of woe came to its sad end, before anyone could pass any further judgement, or make any further jokes at my expense, thankfully Whiff and Andy showed up and much to my relief, at last, the subject changed to the topic of this evening's gig.

In the time it took me to drink another cup of tea, with a bit of persuasion from Dave, Alan kindly leant us his flat back transit van for the night, which meant Andy and Whiff could sit in the cab, instead of being cramped up with the gear in the back of the smaller marina van. Alan gave us his keys, wished us luck and after saying our goodbyes to Ann's kitchen, we loaded our gear onto the flat back and bungee strapped everything down, praying that it wouldn't rain. We all squeezed into the cab and set off on the long journey to the Essex town of Bishops Stortford.

A few minutes into the journey, I was already beginning to feel uncomfortable, it was so cramped inside the cab with the four of us. Dave was in the driver's seat, I was next to him, Whiff wedged in next to me, then Andy at the far end of the bench seat, whose face was flattened up against the near side window, which according to Whiff made his face look a lot better. In such cramped circumstances, it was difficult for Dave to drive, every time he tried to put the long, upside-down L shaped gear stick into first or second gear, my right leg got in the way, causing him to miss the gear and the gearbox would make a horrendous metallic crunching sound, until I got my leg out of the way, and he could ram it home. It was not only uncomfortable; we were finding it hard to breathe, too. Whiff had a theory that if he shaved under his armpits, they wouldn't stink, and so he wouldn't have to waste his money on expensive antiperspirants - rammed up against him now, we knew that theory to be bullshit.

"Dave, please mate, can you wind your window down," I pleaded.

Dave nodded quickly, spinning it down in earnest.

Whiff didn't care, he had something else on his mind, he grinned at the other two mischievously and wriggled a cassette out of his pocket, ramming it into the player on the dash.

"IT'S FUCKING WHISKY TIME!" Shouted the lead singer of Bulldozer out of the console, making everyone crack up laughing

"Oh yes, very good, ha, ha, you bastards," I cried, shook my head, creasing up too, and I thought that night isn't going to go away anytime soon.

A few more miles and more than a few 'It's fucking whisky times' later, after asking for directions, again, more than a few times, we arrived at The Triad, parking up at the back of the decent sized venue and strolled in carrying our gear.

Inside, it looked perfect for bands like us who were just starting out, there was a long well-stocked bar, leading onto a dance floor, and at the opposite end of the venue there was a small, raised stage area, where we would be playing. Once we had got all our gear in and up onto the stage, the Triad's sound engineer wandered over and told us, that we could use The Filthy Habitz Marshall amps if we liked. I said yeah, as long as it was OK with the band, trying not to sound too excited.

"It's fine, they got the amps from a student grant, so they want everyone to use them," said the Triad sound man, smiling broadly at the punk rocker's elated face.

Nice one, I thought, that's the proper punk attitude, everyone helping each other out, not for money, or ego, not for anything, but their conciseness, the goodness in their hearts. I lugged my now redundant Laney amp to the side of the stage, plugged my guitar into the Marsh and let fly with a couple of glorious bar E's, it sounded harsh, guttural, full of menace.

"Oh, wow Whiff, you should use the…" I said, trailing off as I watched him lugging his own amp to the side of the stage.

A moment later, he plugged in, hit a couple of strings, making the stage shudder under our feet.

"Bloody hell, that sounds good, doesn't it?" He enthused.

"Fucking does it," I said, marvelling at its rasping depth.

"OK lads, do you want to do a sound check?" Asked the amused sound man.

I wanted to ask him what he meant as a joke, but instead, I beamed at Whiff like Thames Water had decided to run snakebite through its taps, instead of water.

"Cheers mate, just one track, yeah?"

Sound man nodded, coolly walking off to his little booth at the side of the venue.

A brilliant sounding 'Private War', later he gave us a thumbs up, and we retired to the bar for a couple of snakebites, while we waited for The Triad to open.

A big group of punks pushed in through the double doors at opening time. It was a sight for our sore eyes. Not only was it the most punks we'd seen outside of London, but there were punk girls too, a lot of them, mainly my favourites; the Siouxsie types with their long black spiked up hair, gothic demure, who were a rare sighting outside the sprawling metropolis.

In came groups of skinheads, in their boots and braces, rockers in their Motörhead, Iron Maiden, AC DC t-shirts, followed by more punks, soul boys, hippies, even some New Romantics, had come along to see The Filthy Habitz and us in the process. No excuses tonight, this is our type of audience, I thought, if we don't go down well with this lot, we won't go down well with anybody – oh fucking hell, say if we don't go down well? We get bottled off, or we get hassled, hope Andy puts a lid on it, me too, what are we going to do? I'll just have to write some better tracks, won't I? Oh, fuck!!!

"Hello, hello? Excuse me, excuse me, hello," it was the barman.

"What?" I asked, still lost in thought.

"You're on now" he said, raising his voice above the DJ's set.

"OK mate, cheers," I said nervously, standing up.

I picked up my pint, downed the last of it, surveying my mates, who's expressions told me they were feeling it too.

263

"If we don't go down well tonight, we may as well give up," I said, half joking.

"Yeah, but we are going to Skin," said Whiff confidently. "And you know why?"

"No, mate, go on."

"It's because it's fucking Virus V1 time," bellowed Whiff.

I cracked up laughing, "Fucking is too!"

"Come on lads, let's go and have some fun," said Dave coolly.

"Yeah, that's what I'm going to do," shouted Andy over his shoulder, already on his way to the stage.

"It's fucking Virus V1 time," repeated Whiff, cackling manically.

"Come on, let's blow this place away," I yelled, stepping up onto the stage.

I plugged my guitar into my adopted Marshall and banged the volume right up, hitting a few bar chords, while I surveyed the audience; it couldn't have been any better, a sea of smiling faces, everyone had a drink in their hand, all looking up at us expectantly.

Andy drew the mic up, "Whey… Good evening, we're Virus V1 and you must be our audience."

A couple of cheers came back.

"Cheer's mum, glad you could make it," he said, grinning.

264

"OK, so this is our first number, it's called 'Everybody's Boy'."

Dave hit the intro beat, hit the full kit roll, Whiff and me hit our first notes of the night. It was lift off as we all came in, the Marshall's smashing our sound into the faces of the audience. I smiled broadly, welding the glorious Bar E onto the frets. The wall of sound we were chucking out was incredible; I could see the notes flying through the air into the audience. Then I thought nope, that's probably the whisky from last night still playing tricks on me. I wondered if everyone else was feeling it too, I knew the answer already.

Andy, centre stage, was belting it out, stalking, dropping onto one knee, then rising, pointing his finger accusingly at our enemies in parliament, hammering our message home. Whiff on the left, an oasis of calm, leaning back, riding the beat, totally lost in a world of thumping bass. Then finally Dave. Dave sat in the middle behind Andy, our powerhouse, doing what came naturally to him, doing what he always did; giving the skins a proper drubbing.

One of the floor lights, at the front of the stage was almost blinding me, but at the edges of the burning light I could see a large group of people leaning onto the stage, bopping their heads up and down, grinning, getting it, enjoying themselves. I felt encouraged, feeding off them, so when it came to my solo, controlling my rising adrenaline, I played it like I did in rehearsals, then slid back into the verse smoothly.

'Everybody's Boy' ended to the sound of appreciative applause and a few cheers too.

Andy wiped some of the sweat off his forehead, ran a hand back through his spikes, "Cheers, thank you."

"OK, this next one's for all you Jesus lovers out there! Do you love Jesus?" Andy asked, pointing at a punk girl in front of him, leaning forwards onto the stage.

"Noooo!" She hollered.

"I love you," said a Siouxsie girl standing next to her.

"OK, oh good, er yeah, this next one's called 'Christ Fuckers'!" He said, slightly taken aback.

Dave immediately hit the beat keeping the tempo up. I looked through the blinding light again, saw that the people who had been sitting at the bar, were now standing behind the group around the edge of the stage, some were playfully pushing into them, laughing. Then, as we all came in and the full menace of the track revealed itself, they pogo-ed, slam dancing, pointing at us, nodding their heads back at us. Yes, I thought, they're having as much fun as we are.

A cheers of appreciation greeted us as 'Christ Fuckers' came to its end. I wasn't hanging about; my adrenaline was irresistible, so even before the final note had faded, I launched into 'Protest'. Dave brought us all in with a full kit roll, our Marshall driven sound charged headlong into the crowd, and they reacted by jumping, pumping their fists high into the air. On the second chorus Andy passed the mic out into the audience, they scrambled, grabbing at it, shouting "Stand up, protest if you don't agree," disjointedly.

I smiled turning to Dave, he lifted his up head grinning back, appreciating every second of it and I thought, yes this is what we've been working for over the past year and a half, then got back to it, smashing the chords onto the fret board, reveling in the Marshall's gruff sound.

'Public Enemy' a slow track, was next, the idea being, that it gave people a chance to get their breath back, ready for the mayhem of the faster tracks that were due to follow. I didn't know how hot it was on the dance floor, up here on stage standing in the lights though, I was absolutely dripping with sweat, I was beginning to understand what it was like to be a snake living under a bulb in a tank, so it was good for us to play a slower number. 'Public Enemy' went down well, once again it didn't take the crowd long to learn the chorus, and they were soon shouting, 'Public enemy, public enemy, David McKee', back to us.

A few tracks later, during 'Suffer Little Children' Andy was still full of energy, going for it, dropping to one knee, he sang a line, then jumped up, went to the other side of the stage, rousing the audience over there, audience roused, he ran to the middle of the stage dropped to his knees, like he was the one suffering and bellowed 'Suffer Little Children' into the mic.

A Siouxsie girl, one of the group who had shouted at Andy earlier, grinned at her mates, leant forward, reached out and cupped Andy's bollocks in her hand. Siouxsie's mates shrieked with laughter, drunkenly falling into each other in the mayhem. Andy surprised me and just carried on like nothing was happening, as the girl nurtured his plums; he stayed right where he was for the rest of the track, singing into Siouxsie's mischievous eyes.

Whiff gawped over at them, unbelievingly. I caught his eye, sending us both into hysterics.

I wasn't sure whether we would be allowed to do an encore or not, being the support band, so when Dave hit the massive drum roll at the start of our final number V1 Bomb, I threw everything I had left into it and watched the venue explode before us, people went crazy, jumping, pushing, throwing themselves into each other.

A couple of people at the front went down heavily onto the floor in the complete disorder, only to be helped up by others, who in turn, got knocked down themselves, immediately coming up again, their faces smiling, loving the chaos of it all. I thought, I want to do this forever. I will do anything in my power to make sure that I can do this forever, this is the essence of my life.

In the end, we didn't get our encore, which was a shame, as the audience wanted one as much as we did, so we left them wanting one more. Virus V1 were clapped and cheered as we came off the stage, patted on the back as we walked back through the crowd and with a real thirst on, we lined up the pints of snakebite at the bar and got stuck in.

Andy, Dave, Whiff and me sat back at the bar, quenching our Sahara like thirsts, enjoying the Filthy Habitz, who were pretty good. Then, after their set, we thanked them for the use of their amps, loaded our gear back onto the back of Alan's van and set off for home. Dave drove us back through the had-to-be rainy night, and we talked about playing at The Triad, all agreeing that it had been brilliant to play in front of people who liked real punk rock. We felt like all of our hard work was going to pay off now. Our music and message would be heard after all.

"I reckon a couple more gigs like that, and we'll be on our way," I said, leaning away from Whiff into the draft from Dave's open window.

Dave nodded, "It was brilliant, wasn't it?"

"Andy's already made it, he's a pop star, he's got groupies," said Whiff.

Dave laughed, "Oh yeah, how were her hands, not too cold I hope?"

"No, they were just right," said a grinning Andy.

"Yeah, I bet they are," I cackled, flexing my fingers for effect.

"I'm never going to wash these bollocks again," Andy declared, as we pulled up outside his house.

"What do you mean, again?" Whiff replied, sending us all into fits of laughter.

I sat back, laughing with my mates. I thought music. It heals, it inspires, it unites us, it makes us laugh. It's the universal language, music is the most amazing thing.

The rest is silence.

Printed in Great Britain
by Amazon

81152011R00156